Praise for

"Don't be fooled by the title. This book is a fun-fueled ride filled with wit and wisdom that will propel you toward being a winning woman instead of that nice little girl you were taught to be in childhood."

—Lois P. Frankel, Ph.D.
author of *Nice Girls Don't Get the Corner Office*
and *Nice Girls Just Don't Get It*

"Raw, funny, and inspiring, Happy Bitch gives you an entertaining wake-up call to stop whining and start living! Every woman should read this book."

—Debra Shigley, ESQ
author of *The Go-Getter Girl's Guide*

"Keryl is the kind of smart, savvy, supportive woman you want for your very best friend. Her book is packed with tips that will change your life." —Bonnie Hearn Hill

"I felt like Keryl was speaking directly to my concerns and fears. This is amazing. This is it!" —Diane Fox

"In Chapter 9 alone, I learned more about my relationship with my husband than any other self-help book I've ever read. Really helpful. Truly powerful." —Lisa Allis

"Love, love, love it!" —Kelly Doyle

"I wish every woman would buy this book. I feel as if Keryl has narrated my entire life . . . and added corrections. This is incredible. I'm full of inspiration." —Corie Mulvaney

"One word—fabulous!" —Sarah Hart

"Page after page, Keryl Pesce gives the advice only a girl-friend can share and gets it right every time!" —Jeanne Kelly

"Once you start reading, you won't want to stop. Absolutely amazing. This book kicks ass. Funny, awesome, a must read!" —Cecilia Cook

"Hip, raw and absolutely engaging!" —Denise Panza

"As soon as I started reading, I was hooked. I found myself wanting more. I have a girlfriend who is starting the divorce process. I am buying this for her." —Kathleen Miller

"Keryl is living proof that we possess the strength, courage and determination to change our lives." —Lisa Brennan

"Really amazing!" —Jackie May

"Very well written. It is real. I felt like this book was speaking to me. A real winner." —Elizabeth Gallagher

"Keryl Pesce tells it like it is and holds nothing back. Yet she does it in a way that makes you WANT to change your life around so you become a "Happy Bitch". Yeah Baby! Happiness rules!" —Michele Rybak

"Keryl provides the real-deal DIY Guide for Girlfriends to tap into their true magnificence. Full of practical help from a "Home girl" who's been there." —Robin Diller Torres

"I love the simplicity of the message. My favorite part is the discussion on learning lessons. I firmly believe that everything happens for a reason." —Rebecca Lee

"It really grabbed my attention and interest. Keryl Pesce writes with such enthusiasm and is very charismatic. This is a book I will purchase for many of my friends."

—Jennifer Marchese

"You had me at Happy Bitch!"   —JoAnn Zueckert

"Every female who's experienced life's challenges will relate to this "brass tacks, tell it like it is" practical application book."   —Freda Hamilton

"We weren't handed a "Life Manual" when we were born but, Happy Bitch sure fits the bill. It is a straight forward, easy to read, no-nonsense approach to bringing out the best in all of us, no matter what life throws at us."

—Cheryl Bivona

happy *Bitch*™

The girlfriend's straight-up guide to
losing the baggage and finding the fun,
fabulous you inside . . .

Keryl Pesce

*This book is dedicated to
my incredible husband Craig.*

*This book would not have been possible without your
constant love and unselfish and unwavering support.*

I love you most.

Acknowledgements

To Mom and Dad. No child could ever ask for better parents. You told me I could do anything I put my mind to. You were right.

To my favorite in-laws. For bringing such an amazing man into this world. My life and this book would not be what they are without him.

To Bonnie Hearn Hill. I hoped for the perfect editor. I got her and more. Thank you for your belief in me and this project. You are a consummate professional and beautiful person. Your spunk and determination are off the charts.

To Dave Allis. For helping me dream big. Your generosity allowed me the time to write this.

To James May. For helping me get in touch with my gift. You opened many doors for me.

To Aiden Gallagher. Thank you for trusting me with your dreams. You taught me more than you'll ever know.

To Sam LaBanco Jr. For your generous help with my online presence. You are the master of all web masters.

To Cheryl Bivona. Thank you for your second set of eyes, your loving nudges to keep me going and your constant encouragement.

To my friends and family. Thank you for your continued support and patience while I've been busy. I love and appreciate each and every one of you.

To every Happy Bitch who shared her worries, fears, hopes and personal stories with me. It is because of you I wrote this book. Thank you for the inspiration.

Happy Bitch Martini

2 parts raspberry vodka
1 part amaretto
2 parts cranberry juice
Generous squeeze of fresh lime
Garnish with 2 almonds

This delectable martini represents what a Happy Bitch is about. She's strong, yet sweet. She's delicious, pretty in pink and of course, a little nutty. Why the two almonds? As fabulously feminine as she is, a Happy Bitch has a set of nuts!

Shake this baby good on ice to get it nice and cold and frothy for the best visual effect and taste. Thanks to Leslie Stoddard (www.mixxtress.com) for creating the Happy Bitch. According to Leslie, you should say "Ooh la la!" as you pour your glass of Happy.

Contents

Foreword

by Jonna Spilbor

If we could personify fate, she would no doubt be one really smart chick.

Well, at least that's how she always seems to show up in my life, and the story of how this book landed in my lap—literally—is but one example.

First, the brief back story. My name is Jonna Spilbor. I am a lawyer, television commentator, radio talk show host, writer, and creator of an empowerment workshop series designed to help both men and women get from where they are, to where they want to be. I own my law practice solely and completely. I not only am in a position to give generously to charities, but I've created one of my own. I have no debt. And on top of it all, I am surrounded by loving and wonderful parents, friends and family. I love working out, and am only one size bigger today, than I was in high school (yes, I went from a size 2 to a size 4 and you can bet I'm good with that!)

My life today, is beyond beautiful—a miracle of sorts, if you consider what it looked like a few years ago. You see, I spent many, many years, not just broke—but broken.

It wasn't my fault, of course (sound familiar?) I mean, everything just seemed to *happen to me.* I couldn't afford to pay my electric bill during law school, so I sat in the dark every other month until I found a way to beg, borrow or steal the money to pay the bill. But again, this wasn't my fault. I also totaled a car that my insurance didn't fully cover and bought a jalopy that was towed so frequently for unpaid parking tickets that by the time I scrapped that car, I had paid in parking fines and tow fees TEN TIMES its value! But this wasn't my fault either. I went through boyfriends like Heidi Klum goes through bathing suits until I eventually married a really nice guy who was also broke. We were a perfect match. We got divorced so penniless that my own parents kicked me out of the house I was renting *from them* because I couldn't afford the rent! Guess whose fault that was? Not mine!

I remember one night lying on the floor (actually, I spent many nights lying on the floor so my tears would have a shorter trip to the ground) begging, praying, screaming, punching and doing all the things a person would do if she were utterly miserable. Why? *Because I was miserable.* I was so completely uncomfortable with where I was that I could no longer stand it. I couldn't stand being in my own skin. I couldn't stand being me.

As luck would have it, Fate (the smart chick I mentioned above) was keeping a watchful eye over me and figured I had had about enough (Thanks Fate! I owe you one!) and swooped in for an intervention.

I cannot explain how it happened, and frankly, it doesn't matter. What does matter, is that I started to shift my focus away from all the things I lacked, and—slowly—started looking toward all of the things I had. Believe me, it wasn't much. It started with being grateful for the kind neighbor who ran an extension cord into my apartment so I would have at least one light to study by, thereby moving me out of my makeshift study hall on the building's clothes dryer. I wish I was making this up. At the time, it wasn't much, but even in our darkest moments, we can find a thing or two for which we can be grateful if we simply start looking in the right direction. For me, what I needed to help me shift my focus, was to pull my head out of my ass! No joke.

What happened next is all thanks to the Law of Attraction, which in a nutshell, teaches us that upon which we focus, expands. Focus on being broke, you will stay broke. Focus on earning a nice living, and you will earn a nice living. It sounds overly simple, but truthfully, the formula is not hard. It all starts by shifting your focus to where you want to get to, and then taking some action on it. As you've read a thousand times "Lather, rinse, repeat." Keep repeating the pattern and it will invariably lead you to momentum that will keep you moving in the right direction, and before you know it, you too will be living a life that is beyond beautiful. And guess what? You've already taken the first step. You have picked up this book, and that is all the proof you need to know that you are ready to begin your journey.

Earlier, I referenced that Keryl's book landed in my lap—literally. I say that because at the time I was introduced to *Happy Bitch* (and its author, thee happiest bitch I know!) the then-program director at the radio station where I lend my voice (and have for the last seven years) threw a copy of *Happy Bitch* at me from across the board so I would be prepared to interview Keryl who was to be an upcoming guest on the show. Unfortunately, I wasn't looking when he made the throw, so the book bounced off my shoulder and fell into my lap! Fate, although sometimes a bitch, other times brilliant, indeed has a sense of humor.

I began reading the book that night and simply could not put it down. I immediately recognized what Keryl had managed to do not only with her words, but with her style. She took the Law of Attraction, and "bitchified" it! In other words, she has tailored a very large concept for a very particular audience—women. And she has done so brilliantly.

Whether you need a little help, or a great big shove to begin your personal path from where you are, to where you want to be, *Happy Bitch* is the perfect companion on your trip. Keryl's voice is wise, and witty. Compassionate and intelligent. Straightforward yet sympathetic. But most of all, it is a healthy dose of happy.

I am so very proud to know Keryl personally. She has become my friend, colleague and confidante. And I am proud of you too, dear reader, that you have opened your heart (or your lap) to this beautifully written, invaluable tool on your way to personal growth.

As you open this book, I want you to also open your mind to the prospect that everything is possible for you. I will leave you with two of my favorite phrases. The first, is by Dr. Wayne Dyer, and it is, "When you change the way you look at things, the things you look at change." This book is about to help you do just that.

And the second, is mine.

Just be fearless.

With much love for the author, and for all of you, enjoy this ride.

Jonna Spilbor, Esq.

Introduction

If women didn't exist, all the money
in the world would have no meaning.
~Aristotle Onassis

Have you ever wondered how so much can go so wrong so fast?

It's as if a big ol' dump truck loaded with manure backed up to your front door and unloaded.

"Wait a minute! I didn't order this!" Too late. Before you know it, you're knee-deep in shit without a clue how you're ever going to dig your way out.

Funny thing is, none of us asks for it. It's not like we pick up the phone and promptly request more to worry about. "Hello. Yes, Life? I was wondering if you could send me some problems to deal with. Go ahead and toss in a few unfair surprises while you're at it. Oh, and one more thing. Do you deliver?"

No, that's not exactly how it goes. We don't ask for it, at least not intentionally, and we sure as heck don't deserve it.

But somehow life has a way of piling it on—thicker and deeper than any one person ought to be expected to handle at once. And man, does it ever stink.

I've got news for you sister. It doesn't have to.

The drama, bad luck and raw deals you seem to attract? All that's about to change. Your life no longer needs to be a magnet for bullshit.

Consider what you hold in your hands an intellectual power tool. One which is capable of hauling away a mountain of negativity, guarding against emotional and circumstantial waste and magnetizing your life for happiness and good fortune. Yes, it is possible. How do I know? I've lived it. All of it—joy, happiness, inner peace and of course, all their miserable opposites—heartache, desperation, and immense fear. Which, thanks to the dreaded curse of bad luck happening in threes, I experienced in rapid succession.

Strike one. The president of the company I worked for died unexpectedly. Soon after, his heirs sold the company, and the new owners decided Mexico would be a terrific place to set up shop. Call me difficult, but I disagreed. Although I enjoyed what I did and loved the people I worked with, I decided to jump ship and find a new employer.

Granted, changing jobs isn't the end of the world, but it does pose its fair share of anxiety. It ranks as one of the top four life stressors.

Turns out however, the end of the world was in fact, just around the corner. Shortly after giving notice, I heard the words all wives cherish hearing their husbands say: "I love you."

Only problem was, he wasn't talking to me. Strike two.

I've heard other women describe the experience of discovering their husbands' affairs as feeling as if you've been kicked in the gut. Kicked in the gut? No, it was more like an encore performance of the River Dance, and my insides were the stage. Isn't it amazing how our emotions are capable of literally making us sick? My stomach demanded antacids at a rate that would shame most junkies. Didn't need to worry about cooking. My meals came out of a plastic bottle with a screw top.

"You've got to eat!" my caring family and friends told me.

"No kidding. Tell that to the bilge pump that used to be my stomach."

Ah, but life wasn't done with me yet. Lo and behold, along came strike three. Living with a man who betrayed me and his vows wasn't a place I was interested in calling home, so I packed up and left. The upstairs bedroom of a friend's house became my new home. I tearfully placed all my belongings, one by one, into a closet, one dresser and a single night stand. Lock, stock and barrel, my life, in one room.

It was such a weird sensation. I felt as if I were watching some other chick in a tear-jerker movie. Grab another handful of popcorn, wipe my tears with a tissue, watch the movie, and when it's over, life would be normal again. I guess it was kind of an out-of-body experience. My body was doing things that no part of me wanted to do.

How did I do it? Beats me. I didn't want to leave my husband. I didn't want to leave my home. I didn't want to leave my life. My world, as I knew it, was over, and I was one miserable bitch.

It's been said that life never throws more at you than you can handle. I think that's a load of crap. If you call lying in bed, wondering if my arms could squeeze the pillow any harder or if my eyes would run out of tears, well, then I guess I handled it.

Anger consumed me. I was pissed off at my husband, his mistress and the moron who cursed us all with this "bad luck travels in three" bull. I also had a major beef with life, as if it were some sort of being with a brain capable of plotting against me.

What gives you the right, Life, to hijack everything familiar to me?

I mean, this shit isn't supposed to happen to good people, is it?

It was a completely crazy time. During one of my many moments of desperation, I released my death grip on the pillow long enough to call my husband and beg him to take me back. I know . . . freaking pathetic.

What can I tell you? My emotions were eating me alive, and I felt helpless to stop them. I seriously wondered what God in Heaven I pissed off to deserve dealing with all this at once. Change of jobs, leave my marriage, leave my home—all in a matter of a few weeks. Three out of four of life's top stressors all at once. And if you count the death of my boss, well, there you have it. Four out of four.

There wasn't one shred of familiarity left to my life. Not even me. Who was this angry, bitter woman, feeling so helpless and pathetically sorry for herself? I felt like a stranger in my own life.

Sure, there are women who have dealt with more than I have. But believe me, this was almost more than I could handle.

Or so I thought.

You see, I discovered a little something along the way. We women are pretty amazing creatures. The more challenges life throws at us, the smarter and stronger we become.

Sorry I was so pissed at you, Life. You've turned me into one brilliant chick with a notoriously big set of balls. Thank you for that.

Make no mistake. Inside of us are more resources than any challenges life throws our way. By far.

I sincerely hope you're not in "end of my world as I knew it" mode right now, grieving the loss of a familiar life, but if you are, I want you to understand something. None of what you have experienced, *not one bit of it,* need be in vain. You can absolutely come out stronger and happier on the other side. That is, should you choose to use your experiences wisely. That part is up to you. You'll soon discover how in the pages ahead.

The tough times I had? I can honestly say, without question or hesitation, that I would cry every tear; suffer every bit of agonizing pain again, to be where I am now.

You see, despite the grueling attack on my seemingly perfect life and all-but complete annihilation of my self-esteem, I was able to find my way out of the mess I found myself in. My life now is so vastly different and *better* in every way that

I pinch myself to this day. I went from a pathetic shell of a person, dependent on and married to Mr. Wrong, to a super confident, happy bitch, married to a guy who can't seem to do enough for me. (Yes, they do exist.)

How did I do it? Through the power of choice. And that, my friend, is what this book is all about. Helping you make decisions today that will put you in a better place tomorrow, and the next day and the next. Yes. It means I'm telling you that where you are today is a result of the decisions you made yesterday. I get that may be hard to swallow at first, but hear me out. It may sting a little, but trust me, it's good news.

That infamous Easy Street? The one where all signs point away from you and toward blame? Blame of bad luck, circumstance and other people? Don't go down that road. It's deceiving, and it's nothing but a trap. You'll find yourself in a dark, desperate alley waiting to be rescued. You can scream and cry all you want, but your hero ain't coming. At least not in the form you expect. Why? He's not out there. *She's* in here. Look inside you. *That's* where your hero is.

You see there is a part of you that already possesses all the answers. I mean that sincerely. Taking control of your life, finding your way to a better and happier tomorrow isn't a matter of waiting for something to change or happen "out there". It's about trusting and using the power inside you. I'm going to show you how to do just that.

You've already got what you need. It's just that sometimes we get so overwhelmed we lose faith in ourselves and are unable to see clearly what our next step needs to be. That is until someone who cares about us points us in the right direction and becomes our voice of reason, when our own is suffering from laryngitis.

Right now, that someone is me. I can't change your life. But with a few new pieces of insight, and a slight turn or two, you sure can. No question about it.

Will it be a little scary at times? Perhaps, because it means letting go. It's okay. Just because a certain way of living is familiar, doesn't necessarily mean it is good for you or is what will make you happy. There are times we need to muster up the courage to loosen the grip long enough to reach for something better.

I don't want you to be afraid. I want you to know I will be with you every step of the way with the love and strength hidden in every written word. You will never be alone. I will never be farther away than a turn of the page. Together we are going to lighten your load.

Yes. We are embarking on a journey—one which will allow you to once and for all let go of your heavy and unwanted baggage in exchange for a ticket to a happier place.

Call me crazy, but I feel a sense of responsibility to help you do this. If I have something to offer that will help you live happier and choose not to do anything with it, what does that say about me?

What does that say for any of us for that matter? Perhaps it's about time we drop our guards and judgments. How about we open our hearts—stretch and strengthen our capacity to understand each other. We're far more alike than we sometimes believe. Not the least of which is that every single one of us, you included, has done the best she could with what she had and knew. Aside from everything that makes each of us unique, lies the magnificent strength, kindness and love that makes us the same—that makes us women. We are bound by what unites us to a much greater degree than that which separates us. And it's about damn time we stand up for each other, support each other, build each other up and celebrate the privilege of being a woman.

Let's be done with the days of dismissively touting an unhappy woman as being a bitch as we go on our merry way. We're not bitches. We are amazing people who carry way more burden than we should and who are capable of moving mountains, showing kindness and love beyond compare, and kicking ass when we need to. Let's create a new revolution of today's woman. She's no longer a bitch. She's a *happy* bitch.

By the way, if *anyone* tries telling you life is supposed to be tough, and that happiness is only for the lucky few, drop them the way you would a guy who lies and cheats! They are holding you back out of their own shaded beliefs or fear that you might end up happier than they are. If you can't drop them out of your life, at least stop freaking listening to them.

If the voice telling you that garbage is your own, knock it off. There's enough negativity out there as it is. Quit tossing more on the pile.

Every one of us deserves happiness, even if we've made mistakes. Fuck it. We all have. It doesn't mean you deserve to be punished or unhappy. That's a cop-out. You're afraid of change, of being happy, of loving for fear of being hurt. Not to worry, my friend. You'll soon be over that.

You may be wondering if it's even worth the effort to make changes. Some say happiness is overrated. Try these panties on for size. Every single organ of the human body functions better when we are happy. We feel better, look better, and think better. Our relationships are better. We live longer. We even make more money.

Overrated? Hardly. Our bodies and lives were literally designed for happiness. The way I see it, it's a waste of a human life to give up on or push happiness aside. It's just not how we were meant to live.

Happiness has become my number one priority, upon which all my decisions and choices are made. What contributes to my happiness, I do. What doesn't, I don't. Pretty simple.

Oh, and by the way, I'm not a psychologist. I'm not a therapist. I'm just happy. I'm an average chick who's dug her way out from under a mountain of heartache and climbed to the top. Everything I share with you has contributed to my own happiness.

Besides, I have spent more time than any woman I know studying human behavior. I read so much that my husband calls me a book slut. "You're on to the next one before you even finish the first one," he tells me. Yeah, yeah, yeah. To each her own.

I can't help it. I'm incredibly curious. I am fascinated by what makes us, as humans, as women, tick. Why do we do the things we do? Why do some of us lead lives of endless struggle and others break out and live happy, fulfilling and fabulous lives? Why do some women accomplish great things and others barely tread water?

Why is it that some women are miserable bitches and others are happy bitches?

The answers might surprise you.

As you sow, so shall you reap. It's all about the tiny little seeds planted in your mind. Miserable vs. happy simply depends on what kinds of seeds are planted, how well you feed and nurture them and, of course, how often you pluck out the weeds. That's exactly what we're going to do together.

I'm telling you right now, no, I'm *promising* you right now, no matter what your baggage is, you have the capacity to live happier.

On my road to emotional recovery, I remember telling a friend that my world as I knew it may have ended, but my new world was now in the palm of my hands, waiting to be created exactly as I wished. That's precisely what I did.

I'm here to tell you that you too can live your life by design, not by default. You too are about to find the happy person in you. She's in there. She's in all of us. It's just that sometimes we lose touch with her for a while. You are about to understand why and rediscover how to let her out to play.

As you enjoy the new ideas and empowering thoughts that are about to come to you, relax. Just take it in. Don't worry about searching for a thing. Exactly what you need will come to you. You have my word.

Above all, I want you to remember this. Every single one of us, including you, has done the best we could with what we had and what we knew. Starting right now, my new happy bitch friend, you are about to understand a whole lot more about life, relationships, your feelings, thoughts, struggles and, of course, happiness.

You are about to pack a whole lot more ammunition in your tool belt to kick ass in life. You will be one armed and dangerous happy bitch.

Oh, and by the way, before we go any farther, I want to give you the heads up on a little something. As you read along, you'll notice I call it as I see it and write it as I speak it. That may or may not always be politically correct, but quite honestly, I don't give a crap. This is about two women, sitting down over a glass of wine or cocktail and having a good talk.

Now, if you're okay with that, well, go kick off your shoes, pour yourself a glass of wine or shake yourself up a Happy Bitch martini, and let's talk.

1

---◆---

Bad
Directions

It was when I found out I could make mistakes
that I knew I was on to something.
~Ornette Coleman

Picture this. You are sitting on the living room floor, legs crossed Indian style, your back leaning against the couch. Your baby is standing a few feet away facing you with her arms stretched above her. Her hands are held by your husband, or perhaps one of your parents, or a close friend. She has never before walked on her own. The smile on her face would melt the North Pole in January. Her chubby little legs stomp up and down, anxious to step forward to come to you and your open arms. She has no fear of falling. All she knows is she wants to get to you.

Your arms are outstretched. You call her and encourage her to come. Her hands are freed, and she bounds toward you, one foot after the other, unsteady, and teetering. It takes every effort she has to keep herself upright. She takes her first steps ever, loses her balance and begins to fall. You catch her just before she hits the living room floor.

You hold her out at arms' length, frown, look at her and say, "That's not how you walk. You totally screwed that up. You stink at this. Don't try doing that again until you know exactly how. You should know better."

Then you set her down on the floor and walk away, leaving her confused and fearful of trying again.

Can you imagine any mother responding this way to her child's first steps? No mother in her right mind would ever react this way at a baby's first attempt at walking. Not unless she's on crack.

It's simply not a response that makes any sense or serves any positive purpose whatsoever.

Why? First of all, we have realistic expectations of her abilities, right? Second, this type of negative reinforcement will instill fear in her. It will cause her to be hesitant to grow and learn. Third, you recognize that in order for any of us to become good at anything, we need to give it our best shot first and practice until we master it. Agreed? Good.

Let's go back to the living room floor again. This is more like it:

You squeeze your baby tightly in your arms. You hold her up high in the air, smile a huge smile and tell her, "Good girl! Good job! You took your first steps! I'm so proud of you." You smother her with kisses, sit her down, clap and praise her for what she accomplished.

As you excitedly celebrate your child's first steps, what are you communicating to her? That you are proud of her. That what she did was good. That she should keep trying.

Do you even care about the stumble at the end? No. Of course not. It's not where your attention goes. You pay no mind whatsoever to the fall. The fall is not the point, is it? No. The effort and accomplishment are.

Now as she ventures out throughout her life and attempts to learn and grow, how will she respond? With fear and hesitation? Or with courage, excitement and determination to keep at it until she figures it out? Door number two.

Why? Because that's how you programmed her to respond. She learned from you.

So here's my question. If each of us is perfectly capable of understanding this and communicating this to a baby, why do we have such a hard time doing that with ourselves?

Really. We're notorious for setting unreasonable expectations for ourselves. Then we think we're failures when we don't live up to an impossible set of standards we create. What is up with that?

To expect yourself to be perfect at everything you do, using impeccable judgment in every choice and decision is a classic recipe for an unhappy life. You're setting yourself up.

None of us were born great at anything, except drooling and napping, which, by the way, I have quite perfected as an adult.

Seriously, just suppose we began to look at all our decisions and life experiences as adults the same way we look at a baby learning to walk. Imagine what would happen if we stopped expecting ourselves to be perfect at everything and never fall. How different would your life be if you remembered again how to celebrate every step forward? To focus on the progress and not the mistakes or perceived failures?

I've got news for you. You, me and every other person who ever walked on the face of the planet would be a hot mess if it weren't for our mistakes. Why? We need them to guide us.

Think of it this way. When you buy a new appliance, it comes with a manual. The manufacturer provides you with directions so you know exactly how to use it. Well, where do we get an instructional manual for life? It starts with our parents. They taught us the basics when we were little.

I hate to say this, but maybe Mom was right. Focus on the accomplishment. Forget the mistake. Somewhere along the way, between when our moms praised us for our first steps and we became know-it-all adults, we formed the useless habit of beating the piss out of ourselves for things we screwed up. It's pretty messed up when you think about it.

So if life doesn't come with a manual, how do we know what works and what doesn't? By making mistakes. They *are* life's instructions. They're just written in a secret code. They are invisible until we reveal them. How do we do that? Screw something up. That's how. I'm not suggesting that be your intention. I'm suggesting you be open to the lesson and directions disguised within the mistake.

It's how we learn anything. It started with reading, writing, and building with Legos, and moved on to riding a bike, driving a car, and even being good at relationships. Was my first marriage a mistake? I suppose I could look at it that way. Instead, I choose to see it as my guidance system of how to do better. And I have.

Bottom line, we *need* mistakes to help guide us. Where would you be without them? You'd dig yourself so freaking deep in a hole, you wouldn't see the light of day. No thanks. I'd rather know sooner than later that I need to adjust my course.

We simply need to be willing to get out there, do the best we can with what we have and know and adjust as necessary. Pat ourselves on the back once in a while when we get it right. Now there's a novel idea.

I don't care that you've made mistakes. I sure as heck have. I do care whether or not you use them. That doesn't happen if you sit back and whine and complain or feel sorry for yourself, or beat yourself up because you screwed up. Give me a break. Who hasn't? It's part of life.

"Yeah, but I've made some pretty big mistakes. I have a hard time letting go of it. I should have known better."

Oh really? Maybe not. What if I told you it wasn't your fault?

Remember when we were little and had imaginary friends? It was actually pretty cool. We played with her and had imaginary conversations with her. She was our constant companion, ready whenever we needed her.

Then we grew up and got stupid. We abandoned our imaginary friend because, "Adults don't do those things." Imaginary people don't really exist.

Or do they?

The fact is, they do. You are one woman, but there are actually two parts to you. There's the conscious you and there's the subconscious you. Now I realize that the fact that you have a subconscious mind isn't news to you, but what I'm about to say probably is.

Your subconscious self (formerly known as your imaginary friend) is the source of your mental and physical habits and behaviors. Read that again if you need to. This is a juicy nugget you just might want to gnaw on for a minute.

Ever wonder why people seem to make the same mistakes over and over? It's as if they are their own worst enemies, isn't it? Have you ever talked with someone until you were blue in the face, giving her all the logic in the world to help her see why she shouldn't be doing what she was doing but nothing changed? Do *you* have habits or behaviors that you *know* aren't good, yet you can't seem to change them?

Do you want to know why? Drum roll please.

Because our habits and behaviors are driven by our subconscious. Why is that important to know? *Because if our subconscious controls and directs our habits and behaviors, all the logic in the world can be dumped on our conscious mind and it'll slide right off.* It doesn't reach us where it needs to. In the battle between conscious and subconscious, the subconscious will always win. Make no mistake, that baby is behind the wheel. That's who is driving you around.

It's the reason why we do things that don't make sense to us—because they have nothing to do with sense. It's "nonsense" my friend. It's why you can read book after book about self-development and improving your life situation, but when you are finished reading, despite a few attempts, you don't see long-term change. It's why you decide on a conscious level you want to lose weight, but can't seem to stick to a diet and exercise regime. We are attempting to alter our behaviors intellectually, and that is not where real change happens.

Real change happens when we reach ourselves on a subconscious level. How do you do that? It's easier than you think, and I will show you. But you'll have to wait until the next chapter for that.

First, there's something you need to understand. And that is how the subconscious gets its instructions—how it knows in what way to direct your behavior. Its original set of instructions didn't come from you.

Remember how I told you my first husband had an affair? Well, guess what? Unbeknownst to me, it was destined to happen. Why? Bad directions. When I was a kid, my father cheated on my mother. I was aware of it.

Even though I didn't like how it affected my mother, that experience became an instruction to my driver. You see, we are drawn subconsciously to what is familiar to us—especially that which happens in our childhood. Good or bad. It doesn't matter.

When I mentioned in the introduction that we need to open our hearts and stretch our capacity to understand each other, this is what I meant. None of us chooses where and to what family we are born. We don't choose the people and circumstances that affect us when we are little. Whether I'm born in upstate New York to a poor family and you're born in Bumfuck, Missouri to a family who owns half the state, we all have different experiences that shape our thoughts and behaviors—that direct our driver.

Think of it this way. We all go through life as little baggage handlers. Since the time we were little, we were handed more and more to carry. Some of it was healthy and served to encourage us to be the best we could and live the best life we could.

Unfortunately, much of what we were handed does the exact opposite. It weighs us down, and holds us back. Everything we see, our opinions, actions, decisions and *results*, are all filtered by what's in those bags. It's why certain people do things you'd never do. It's why you do things other people would never do. It's why six people can look at a situation and each one has a different take. Because each of us has different belief systems we're carrying around, and they become our individual filters, our point of view. Some, more warped than others.

That is exactly why you will find people who seem to be their own worst enemies. I'm telling you. They can't help it. They haven't got a clue they're carrying around someone else's baggage.

Our parents, teachers, friends, our friends' parents, aunts, uncles, coaches, all gave us a little something to carry. The majority of our belief systems are programmed into us before we have a chance to choose whether or not they serve us. Some are intentionally given to us, such as religious beliefs, but many are unknowingly placed in our bags by people who care about us.

I saw my father cheat. I grew up believing men cheat. I married a man who cheated. As the saying goes "The apple doesn't fall far from the tree." This is why. Do both my parents love me and care a great deal about my well being? You bet your ass they do. It wasn't their fault they handed me unhealthy beliefs. They didn't know any different. Parents don't sit down one day, scratch their head and say "Let's see. How can I fuck up my child for life?" No. They're working off their own misguided directions doing the best *they* know how.

What's the significance of this? It means the end of beating yourself up for the mistakes you've made or the failures you've had. *They had nothing to do with your intelligence or character.* You just had a misdirected driver. She was working off of some bad directions.

I'm not sharing this with you so you can go off blaming someone else for your misfortunes. That's not it at all. I'm explaining this to you so you better understand the source of our behavior. In doing so, I'm handing you the ability to once and for all, forgive yourself for past mistakes. Just as important, I'm handing you the ability to forgive others in your life.

Still hanging on to resentment that your parents should have acted differently than they did? Time to let go of it. I'm not saying they did everything right. I'm saying you have no clue what kind of baggage they are carrying. Nor does anyone else know what kind of baggage you are carrying.

Remember we talked about making better choices? Here's a biggie. *You don't have to carry the baggage around anymore.* You can look at what was given to you and choose whether or not it is good for you. If it isn't, stop carrying it. Set it down. Walk away. Let it go. Pull out the weeds. Plant new seeds.

You have the opportunity in your lifetime to alter the course of future generations. You see how beliefs, habits and behaviors are passed down from generation to generation. You see the positive impact you can have on your own life. But how about this? What kind of impact can you have on future generations? Imagine the power one person has.

Do you want to know why I chose this as the first topic to talk about? It's entirely possible that the reason you aren't happier than you are is you feel you don't deserve it. What if there is a part of you that thinks you have a debt to pay, that you owe it to the world to be miserable because you've made mistakes? Then what happens? *You* end up stuffing even more junk in your already overloaded bags. How so? Negative self talk.

Bring the image to mind for a moment of those you love, very, very much. Maybe your daughter or son, your husband or lover, maybe your mother or grandmother. Let me ask you something. Would you ever call them names, insult them or put them down? Not likely.

Then why do we do it to ourselves?

Recently, one of my girlfriends was on a mission to lose weight, and I was checking with her on her progress. I sent her an e-mail and asked her if she exercised that day. She replied back and wrote "No, I didn't. I suck. I'm a loser." Those were her exact words.

What was she doing? She was talking trash to herself, wasn't she? Well, guess what? She's stuffing more weight (no pun intended) in her bags. How many times have you done this to yourself?

I sent a note back telling her she was one of the smartest, most thoughtful, hardest working, and physically beautiful women I know, and it's true. She is. I pointed out what she was doing, and it really opened her eyes. She wasn't aware of what she was doing to herself.

We're all guilty of talking to ourselves in a way that we would never talk to someone we love. We're giving our subconscious bad ideas. We're giving our driver bad directions. We're building and reinforcing our own negative self image. And that, my friend, is something a happy bitch doesn't do.

If there is one person you should love and honor more than anyone in the world, it is you. Can we really expect other people to respect us if we don't first respect ourselves? It begins with us. There's your hero. She can be your ally or your enemy. Which do you prefer?

If you get just one message from this book (I sure hope you'll get a lot more than one), I want you to get this: *Every person, including you, deserves happiness.* I don't care what you've done in the past. If there are apologies to offer that will make you feel better, go for it, but whatever you do, stop beating yourself up.

It's time to give yourself permission to be happy again. The time is now to finally begin freeing yourself of unnecessary baggage, so just drop it. Forgive yourself and let's get happy.

Lose this:

Guilt over past mistakes and self-inflicted criticism.

Choose this:

*Accept you've done the best you could with what you had
and what you knew. Forgive yourself
and give yourself permission to be happy.*

2

◆

Brand New
Directions

*Unhappiness is not knowing what we want
and killing ourselves to get it.*
~Don Herold

Is there anything you want to do or accomplish but can't seem to get the results you want? How about wanting to lose weight, but can't? Find the right person? Become wealthy?

How would you like to change that? Imagine if you were suddenly able to set your sights on what you want to accomplish and once and for all, just do it.

That, my friend, is exactly what you will be able to do by the end of this chapter.

Remember that driver we talked about in the last chapter? Your imaginary friend you've brought back to life? There's a little something about her I haven't told you yet. She does something most of bitches don't do. She takes orders.

To get yourself to do what you've been unable to until this point, all you need to do is give your driver better directions. That's it. It begins by letting her know precisely what you want.

"Yeah but, I already know what I want."

Do you really? Maybe you don't. The majority of the time I ask women what they want, it usually goes something like this:

Me: "Well, what do you want?"

Woman: Silence.

She can't answer me right away. Do you think that could be part of the problem? Hello? How will you ever discover happiness if you aren't crystal clear on what it is you are even looking for? Back to the conversation.

When they finally do answer, I get responses like this:

"I don't want to work at my job anymore."

"I'm tired of struggling with money."

"I hate all this stress in my life."

"I wish I wasn't carrying this extra weight."

Can you spot the pattern?

I then repeat the question. "What do you want?"

Here's where they look at me like I've got three heads. "I just told you."

"You just told me what you *don't* want." I'll tell them. Pause. "I'm not sure I'm following you."

Are *you* following me? What you *want* is worlds apart from what you *don't want*. They're not even in the same universe.

All unhappiness is caused by us wanting circumstances to be different than what they are now. Whatever it is—a husband who helps without being asked, a boss who isn't a prick, bigger boobs, tighter ass, whatever. There's nothing wrong with wanting more or something different. We'll get into that in more detail in a later chapter. The problem isn't in the wanting. The problem is in the method of thinking. Most people spend the bulk of their time thinking about what's *wrong*. We even go in search of reasons to justify our misery.

How many times have you seen it yourself? Have you ever had a friend or relative complain about what sucks about her life and as you offer potential solutions, she defends her right to be miserable? People wear their problems as some sort of badge of honor. "Look at me. My life is fucking miserable. Let me tell you why." No thanks.

Make a note. **What we focus on expands.**

How can your circumstances improve if all your energy and thoughts are wrapped up in what's wrong and what you don't like? They can't.

If you want your life to be easier, more relaxed, more ful-filling and happier, all you need to do it give your driver bet-ter directions. If you don't, she doesn't know where to take you. It's like hopping in the back of a limo and telling her all the places you *don't* want to go. You're in the back seat pulling your hair out with your fists screaming "Get me out of here!" She's looking back at you in the rear view mirror saying "Yeah, and?"

She doesn't have a clue where to take you. So what hap-pens? She stays put. You stay put. Nothing changes. There you are scratching your head wondering why the heck you're still parked in Shitsville.

Your driver will take you wherever it is you tell her to take you. She literally is your servant. The key is properly communicating with her. How do you do that? Speak to her in terms of what you want. You see she isn't capable of un-derstanding negation.

When you say "I don't want to work at my job." She hears "Work at my job." When you have repeated thoughts or conversations about what you don't want, all she hears and recognizes is the subject matter. "Work at my job . . . feel overwhelmed . . . not enough money . . . too much weight . . . too much stress." So where is she going to take you? Right to the heart of Stress, Fat and Poor Town, USA. Do not pass "Go". Do not collect $200.

When I was going through my divorce, there was a pe-riod of time when all I wanted was not to feel pain, not to feel like my world had caved in on top of me. That may have been a normal part of the grieving process, and it's okay for a reasonable period of time, but it wasn't going to get me to happy. Not until I changed my focus.

Why? *When you change your focus, you change your results.* Plain and simple.

Ever hear the expression that today's problems cannot be solved with the same level of thinking that created them? This is exactly what it refers to.

Your world is about to change, my friend. You are about to shift your focus and give your driver some brand-spanking-new directions. Let's get rolling.

I want you to imagine you could have anything. Just put aside for a moment any limiting thoughts—not enough money, not enough time, not smart, brave or lucky enough, whatever, just put those aside. Let's go to that place in your mind right now where anything is possible. Which by the way, is a fantastic place for you to hang out. I visit it often.

Now that you are there, what is it you would love to see changed about your life? About yourself?

Take a moment now and go get yourself a piece of paper and a pen. Create two columns. On the left, write down exactly what circumstances you would like to see different in your life. For example, "I would like to have plenty of money to live comfortably, travel and take care of those I love."

The second column is what behaviors you currently have that you would like to change. For example, "I would like to get myself to exercise five days a week."

Okay? So the first column is situational or circumstantial. The second column is behavioral. You may end up with items in one column that tie into the other column. For example "I want to be thin and toned." could be in your left column. "I want to eat healthy and exercise regularly." could be in the other column. Remember, write out what you want, not what you don't want.

Stop reading now and do this exercise.

Welcome back. Congratulations. You just did more than 90% of the population by giving yourself a clear target. It never ceases to amaze me how many people want more but aren't willing to do what it takes. Especially when it's as simple as taking two minutes, applying a little thought and writing something down. Nice work.

Now, a little more about your subconscious. Yes, she is capable of directing your behavior. What you may not realize is she is also capable of impacting the universe in which you live. She has the capacity to take your thoughts and from them, manifest reality. Given proper direction, she can literally magnetize your life.

If you are hearing this for the first time, it may feel a little far-fetched. Let me remind you that every last shred of advice I give you I have applied and benefited from. Open your mind and believe.

That's *what* she is capable of doing. Now let's talk about how to get her to do it.

Let's start by addressing your own behaviors you'd like to change.

When you behave in a way you wish you wouldn't, such as over-indulging in food or arguing with your children or spouse, you didn't consciously choose that response. You think you did, but you didn't. Your subconscious did.

Here's how it works. Your subconscious directs your habits and behavior. We already established that. The way she does that is by responding to triggers. A trigger can be something someone else does or says, such as your husband leaving the toilet seat up. Or it can be a thought or feeling inside you, such as thoughts of being inadequate in some way. In a split second, she searches your database of memories to see how you responded in the past, serves that up, and you react.

The more times that process happens, the more deeply ingrained the behavior becomes and sometimes even grows intense or extreme.

For example, the first time your husband leaves the toilet seat up, it may be mildly annoying. Ten years later, you want to flush his head in the damn toilet for doing it. Am I right?

Pay attention the next time you act in a way you wish you didn't. *What happened the instant before that?* There's your trigger.

Here's the good news. To create better habits and behaviors, all you need to do is build in more productive responses to the triggers. Since your current responses are merely based on memories of past responses, just give your subconscious new memories to draw from.

Here's the really cool part. *The memories don't need to be real.* You see your driver cannot tell the difference between reality and imagination. To her, it's all the same.

Do you realize what this means? You can create whatever behavior you want by imagining yourself doing it first. Here's how.

As I just mentioned, first look for your triggers. There's your point of departure. Once you see what they are, visualize yourself responding in a way you prefer—one that serves you better. If its ten years later, and your husband still leaves the toilet seat up, he probably is not going to change his habits. Certainly, not as a result of you bitching at him. More on that later. So rather than wasting your energy wishing *he* would change, which by the way, you have virtually zero control over, change your response. Change what the trigger causes you to do and feel.

All you need to create a new behavior is to visualize yourself acting out that behavior two to five minutes a day, twice a day for twenty-one days. Why twenty-one days? That's all it takes to form a new habit. Find someplace quiet and comfortable. Slip away into that place where all things are possible. See the trigger. Visualize your new response. Imagine what that new response does for you.

After twenty-one days (or sooner), a new habit will be formed, and the new behavior will become your new automatic response. Hot stuff, isn't it?

Try it with something small first. Build in your new habit, see how easy it is to do, then move on to the next behavior you'd like to change. If you miss a day, no sweat. Remember, we're done with beating ourselves up. Just pick up where you left off.

Next, let's magnetize your life. It works in much the same way—through visualization. As you'll see in a minute, you already know exactly how to do this.

To create a new and better reality, you need to see it in your mind first. Feed that data to your driver, and she will take you there. See it often and clearly enough in your mind first, and your subconscious will think it is something already in existence. She will direct your behavior, the behavior of others around you, circumstances and opportunities in alignment with your vision. The key is to be consistent and persistent and feel the energy and emotions associated with the vision being reality. You look in the mirror and your shoulders are toned and strong. Your waist is thin. Your stomach is flat. That's the vision. Now think about what that feels like. Get in touch with that feeling. It's a giant human magnet.

You want more money? Visualize yourself receiving, enjoying and deserving more money. You will see results with as little as four to ten minutes a day, but go ahead and do this as often as you like—even while you're engaged in other activities like drying your hair, washing the dishes or trying to fall asleep.

I told you earlier you already know how to do this, and that's the truth. In fact, many people, women especially, do this virtually all day long. The only problem is they are visualizing the wrong stuff. It's called worry.

The most significant defining difference between miserable bitches and happy bitches is how they direct their thoughts. Period. You now know precisely how to do just that. Imagine the possibilities. Just think of how much power you now have.

The exciting part is the results of new and better-directed thinking are almost instantaneous. The second you decide what you want, and begin focusing your thoughts on that, you will create an entirely new energy to feed all your decisions and actions. That energy is magnetic. All of a sudden, life becomes easier. Your reality is transformed because your thoughts have been transformed.

Make no mistake. *Reality follows thought.* The majority of unhappy people believe the opposite. "My thoughts are a result of my reality." That pattern of thinking is like hopping in the back of a car, and letting someone else drive you wherever they choose. You're not going to do that. You get to control and direct your thoughts. You are going to give your driver crystal clear directions.

As you open and expand your mind and the possibilities, you will stumble upon a thought or an idea and get butterflies in your stomach. That, my friend, is your driver revving your engine. When you get that feeling, you know you are on to something. That's energy and it's very real. That's a big-ass road sign for your driver directing her to "Drive exactly here."

Everything I've just described is exactly how I created the reality I now live. Exactly. I decided I wanted a man who could cook—who made me feel like a better me when I was around him—who spoke highly of me whether I was in his presence or not. A few years ago, it was only a thought in my head. Today, it's my reality.

What do you want tomorrow's reality to be for you?

Decide what you want. Keep thinking in terms of what you are *reaching for*, not getting *away from*. See it in your mind first. Reality will follow. It's time to live again, laugh again, be happy again. Let life become an exciting adventure. Don't worry about life letting you down. That's simply an old, unhealthy pattern of thought. It doesn't serve you. Let's talk about that next . . .

Baggage Drop

Lose this:
Focusing on what you don't want and worrying about all that can go wrong.

Choose this:
Focus on what you do want and imagine yourself doing, being and having whatever that is.

3

◆

Most people would rather be certain
they're miserable, than risk being happy.
~Robert Anthony

If you're like me, somewhere on your body, you've got a scar or two hanging around as a reminder of an old injury. Some of mine have been with me since I was a kid. A skinned knee or two, a nasty splinter or piece of glass stuck in my foot from running around barefoot when I wasn't supposed to. Each one tells its own story. If the cut wasn't too bad, Mom patched us up with a Band-Aid or two, kissed the pain away and sent us back out to play. After a while, those scars faded and became barely noticeable, unless, of course, we'd done a good enough number on ourselves and needed stitches. That baby might never fade away completely.

It's pretty amazing when you think about it—how our bodies work, that is. When we suffer a cut, our body knows there is a part of us that needs help and goes to work instantly. It fights off dangerous bacteria and immediately begins the growth of new cells, like some sort of invisible army of soldiers, protecting the borders of our body. As we heal, scar tissue forms to protect the vulnerable area. If the injury was severe enough, and nerves were damaged, we're left with not only an ugly scar, but a place on our skin that is actually numb. Kind of ironic, considering a spot that once experienced pain now can't feel anything at all. Seems a little extreme, doesn't it?

You know what else is ironic about it? We may not be skinning our knees anymore, but we haven't escaped the risk of forming scars that end up numbing us to feeling. How so?

What happens when we suffer a tough emotional experience? We put up a protective wall—a barrier between our heart and the outside world.

When you have a painful life experience such as divorce or loss of a loved one, you also suffer an injury. Except this time, your emotions have taken a hit. They become your vulnerable spot. So what happens is an emotional wall of scar tissue forms around your heart. In an effort to ease the pain and protect against future injury, you become emotionally numb. How? You stop hoping. Stop dreaming. You lower your expectations and become emotionally callused and scarred. Just as with your skin, the worse the injury and more severe the pain, the thicker the scar tissue.

You might think your emotional scars aren't as bad because they are invisible. No one can see you've been hurt, right? Wrong. The fact is, they do show, big time. They show in your actions and in your attitudes. They show in your face. Have you ever looked in the eyes of another woman and felt her pain? She doesn't need to tell you. You sense it. Her eyes tell you "I've been hurt. Stay away from my heart. Don't get my hopes up. I won't risk being disappointed or hurt again. Leave me alone." Maybe you see it in your own eyes when you look in the mirror.

So here's my question. Is the way to survive past pain to live a present and future emotionally numb? Is that really the answer?

There's a common misconception about what has happened in the past. We believe and act as if it has power over us. The fact is the past has *zero* power over us. None. Zilch. Nada. It's not the past that affects us. It's the baggage of old thoughts we carry around that have any effect on us.

The past is done, isn't it? It exists only as a memory. The only power it has is the power we choose to give it by continuing to play the same tapes over and over in our heads. Who gets to choose what we think? We do. Who then decides whether or not the past affects our present? *We do.*

Here is where emotional scar tissue differs from physical. *We get to choose whether or not it stays.*

Lowering our expectations to avoid pain is a choice we make. And what does that get us? Life in prison. That's what. Your cell may not have four walls and a concrete floor, but nonetheless, you're shut off from the outside world.

How many of us have chosen to do that to ourselves? And at what cost?

Nothing on the outside can hurt us because nothing can reach us. We've put our guard up and the guard is us. We think we're safe, but the irony is, we're slowly committing emotional suicide. It's not the past experience that's killing us. *It's our own reaction to it that is killing us.* In our attempt to avoid pain, we end up living a sad, lonely, and bitter existence.

You've got to wonder why any of us would choose to live this way. It's so screwed up. Are we a few fries shy of a happy meal? Or are we simply unaware we even have a choice in the matter at all?

I told you right from the beginning that life is all about choices. This is a big one. Whether or not you continue to live in a state of perpetual sadness behind a false sense of security is up to you. You decide whether or not the scars of the past stay or go.

Letting your guard down could be a scary thought for you. You don't want to be hurt again. Who does? The truth is, as long as you keep your guard up, you're subjecting yourself to a different sort of pain. One that is with you every day. Your screwed up way of dealing with past pain is to keep it alive by not forgiving it. Seriously. Think about that. You're doing exactly the opposite of what you set out to do—avoid pain. Instead, you prolong the life of the pain and keep it alive. That's precisely what you do when you don't forgive the person or situation and move on. That's a pretty heavy weight to carry with you every where you go. So why do it?

I know what it's like to be hurt. I put my heart in the hands of someone who stomped the piss out of it. Do I ever want that to happen again? Not in this lifetime. However, I choose not to live in fear of it. I choose not to allow something from the past to dictate my present or my future.

Could I get hurt or burned again? Yes. I'm not telling you that you won't either. You might. You might not. I honestly don't know. I do know this. You will be a lot worse off choosing a life absent of hope, excitement and love. Why? The risk of what you are missing and regretting what could have been is a hell of a lot worse than the risk of being hurt again.

I promise you this. When you are at the end of your life, your regrets will be about what you *didn't* do, not what you did.

Life is a beautiful thing. It always has been and always will be. It hasn't stopped being beautiful. You just might not see it because your emotional scar tissue is blocking the view. Do you ever wonder what's out there that you're missing? I'll tell you what. Life. Love. Opportunity. Miracles. They are all right there, waiting for you to let them in.

Let's put aside for a moment what you might be missing and ask a different question. What are *you* holding back from the rest of the world?

Think of it this way. You are a lot like a pearl. No two pearls are exactly alike, and that's what makes them and us so precious. The pearl begins its life as a tiny speck of sand, unnoticed and seemingly insignificant. It lives the first part of its life cultivated in soft, nurturing tissue receiving everything it needs to grow and form into something beautiful.

But it also lives inside of a very tough, hard, resilient shell; the oyster. The oyster does the job it needs to for the time necessary and eventually opens up and releases the beautiful pearl to the world. It's pretty scary for the pearl to leave the safety of its shell. It's lived with the same surroundings for so long that it's comfortable, even though its world is tiny and dark. You've got to wonder what the pearl is missing if it stays inside its shell. Just as important, what is the world missing?

Somewhere out there, someone's life is waiting to be touched by the pearl. Just how or in what way isn't certain, but one thing is for sure. As long as it stays in its shell, someone is missing out.

You, your soul, your presence is meant to be shared with the world. It's not just about what *you* are missing. What are the *rest* of us missing? You have gifts and talents that are uniquely yours, or there would be no reason for you to be here. Did you know that at conception, odds can be in excess of one in *one hundred million* that you would be the exact person created? Think about that.

Every single one of us is here for a reason. What's yours? What gift do you have to give the world? Who or what is out there in need of you?

For you this might be a bigger part of the equation. Perhaps you don't yet see your significance. I promise you this. Whether it is thousands, millions, or just one, someone is waiting to be touched and affected by your presence.

Maybe you've lived too long, feeling small and insignificant, like that grain of sand, not realizing you've grown into something spectacular and perfectly unique.

Who is out there waiting for you to come alive, venture out and touch their lives? Perhaps a child waiting to be conceived or one needing a mom to love her or an old woman whose reason to smile becomes you. Maybe there's a book in you waiting to be written that will forever impact the lives of millions. You will never know until you venture out, until you choose to get rid of the scar tissue and step out of your shell.

How do you do it? It starts, as always, with a choice. In this case, of how to view your past experiences.

You can choose to look at them as unfortunate, something that should have been different, and as if someone or the world has done you wrong. That, my friend, is what I call baggage. Or you can lose the baggage and look at every past experience as having served its purpose, to shape and strengthen you and point you in a better direction.

The truth is I don't know if I would appreciate the relationship I have now with my husband if I hadn't had a bad experience the first time. I doubt I would. Maybe it was all part of the master plan to begin with. What if it was all a prelude to set me up perfectly to enjoy right now to the fullest?

That's what I choose to believe. As a matter of fact, I now live with that assumption. It's how I've come to see all experiences. From the major events like my divorce to certain days when it seems every little thing goes wrong, I assume they're all there to help me.

Life is a lot like the weather. We complain when it rains as if life would be perfect if it were sunny every day. But do you know what you get with all sun and no rain? A freaking desert. That's what you get. Who wants that?

In life we need a little rain sometimes. I know it sounds like a cliché, but I think we forget. Rain is nature's way of working with the sun so all forms of life can thrive. *Rainy days are a necessary part of the deal.* We need them to grow and thrive.

When you are going through a tough time, you need to trust that life is giving you exactly what you need. What happens too often is most of us are blind to it. We bitch and complain and fight the balance of life. We live from the assumption that we're getting a raw deal, that life is unfair, when precisely the opposite is true. Life gives us exactly what we need.

As you start to look at tough times this way, they won't seem so tough anymore. You'll see them for what they are—a necessary part of a meaningful life.

Changing how we view past experiences is the first step in removing the scar tissue. The second is . . .

Baggage Drop

Lose This:

*Keeping past pain alive by leaving
emotional scar tissue in place.*

Choose This:

*Let go of past hurts. They're over with.
Come alive again and let the world around you
benefit from your being a part of it.*

4

Forgiveness Gives You Control

*If there were in the world today any large number
of people who desired their own happiness
more than they desired the unhappiness of others,
we could have a paradise in a few years.*
~Bertrand Russell

When you were little, did you ever worry about monsters
hiding under your bed or in the closet, waiting for the perfect
moment to scare the piss right out of you? I used to wonder
if they really existed. Until I was seven. Then I had proof.

Well, sort of. My monster wasn't quite what you would
imagine. It wasn't furry or ugly. As a matter of fact, I couldn't

see it. I could only hear it. You see, my monster was a conversation I wished I hadn't heard. I know that sounds odd, but if something is capable of ripping apart your insides, that's a monster in my book.

"He can go jump in a lake for all I care!" Someone on the other end of the phone was getting an earful from my mother. "Who knows where he is or who he's with? I don't care anymore." Seemed to me by the way she was crying she cared an awful lot.

Enter monster. Moms aren't supposed to cry. They make tears go away, don't they? First certainty of my childhood world that suddenly wasn't so certain anymore. Santa Claus would be the second.

Now, I may have been so young that I still made forts out of blankets and drank my milk through a Twizzler with both ends bitten off, but I was old enough to put two and two together. I figured out quickly enough why she was upset. Dad was somewhere he shouldn't be, and wherever he was or whoever he was with, it was ripping my mother apart. Not to mention the number it was doing on me.

"Go back to bed!" she told me abruptly. Her sharp command startled me. I don't think she expected me to be standing there listening to her conversation. She wasn't the only one. Only a few seconds before, I decided to go back to bed before she saw me. Apparently, my feet had another plan. They took my ass right into the kitchen where she sat on the phone.

"Are you okay, Mommy?"

"I'll be fine. Go back to bed."

Apparently, she had more influence over my feet than I did. They turned me around and took me and my monster back to bed.

As I lay trembling underneath the covers and praying for sleep to make it all better, I vowed never to do what my father had just done to my mother—and unknowingly, to me.

It became a firmly grounded principle, upon which my grown-up self would operate.

From the time I started dating, I chose to be faithful. To me, whether married or not, the situation required the same respect. A piece of paper didn't dictate how I acted. My principles did.

Many years later, as I overheard for the second time in my life, a conversation I wish I hadn't, the very foundation upon which I built my life disintegrated into a pile of rubble.

"I don't care. I love you. I love you, baby and I'm going to be with you." my husband said.

He had no idea I was standing right behind him as he spoke the words to his lover on the other end of the phone.

I don't know if you've ever been in a similar situation, but I'll tell you what. It's one of the worst kinds of pain possible. Why? Because sometimes shit happens in life, and there's no apparent reason. Someone gets sick, seriously hurt or dies. Sometimes it just happens. The pain is tough enough. Top it with actions someone *chose* to take, that rips your heart to shreds. It's so hard to wrap your head around it. Especially when the person who made the choice was the one who promised to love and protect you for life.

Seventeen words, and my life had changed forever.

My friend cradled a sobbing me in the back of her car as her husband drove us away from the crowd and away from a life that would never again be the same.

It was the beginning of grieving the loss of my life as I knew it. And you know what was the most screwed up part of it all? Here this guy just completely destroyed my world, and all I wanted was his arms to comfort me. I was quite sure I was losing my mind.

For the first time in my life, I met with a therapist. Proudly, I told her I was doing a pretty good job keeping every minute of the day busy so I wouldn't have to think—so I wouldn't have to feel pain. I'll never forget what she said.

"Keryl, in order for this to get better, you just have to go through it. You can't go around it, under it, or over it. You just have to go through it. If you feel you want to grab a blanket, curl up in bed and just cry, then go do it. Just don't stay there all day."

No need to tell me twice. I cried so hard my sides ached for two days.

If you've ever been there, you understand the classic battle between logic and emotion. They are at complete odds. Make no mistake. At first, our emotions rule. Logic is temporarily out of the picture.

A little time does wonders, though. With each passing day, my emotions settled down, and the logical part of me began to step up to the plate. I had some decisions to make.

I could go one of two directions with this. I had every right to be angry and pissed, wouldn't you agree? I could have figured out any number of ways to completely bust his balls and make his life miserable. In fact, it's the normal knee-jerk reaction for most women. Start the proverbial pissing contest. Game on!

Except where does that get you? Where most pissing contests get you—covered in piss. He'll take your shit for only so long before he tosses it back. Now you're both playing a losing game. One of you figures a way to get back at the other and vice versa. Down the spiral you go. Deeper and deeper into an abyss of misery. Farther and farther away from what both of you want—to move on and live happy again.

Have you ever seen women celebrate little victories because they found ways to get back at their exes? Too often, right? All they're doing is stepping right smack into a trap, one that is certain to confine them to a life of anger and resentment.

Could I have gone down that road easily enough? Sure. I had reason enough to be angry. But what would that get me?

How about taking a different road? The higher road. How about accepting the situation as it was and make it the best it could be? There's an interesting concept. Isn't that what we should be doing every moment of every day? Imagine the difference it would make in our lives if we constantly asked ourselves "How can I make this the best it can be?" instead of "Why me?" The latter is useless.

You're fooling yourself if you think hurting someone else will make you feel better. Sure, you may get some initial short-lived satisfaction for evening the score, but it doesn't last. I'm all about making decisions that make me feel good about myself, smart, in control and confident. Does purposely hurting someone else back do any of that? Not in this lifetime. Otherwise, you're no better than he is, are you?

Granted, it took me a couple of weeks to reach the decision. Once I did, I was sure I had made the right choice. Here's what I told him. "Look, there is enough pain and hurt associated with this whole thing. Let's not make it worse. Let's not fight."

We didn't.

Think about what I was able to do. *I took control of an out-of-control situation.* I couldn't control him or what he had done. I could, however, control how I handled it. Did I have every right to want to hang him from the ceiling by his nuts? Yeah, and I admit the thought crossed my mind a time or two early on, but what for? What would that do for me?

Pay close attention here. Choose your responses based on what you want them to do *for* you, not *against* him or whoever it is you feel wronged by. It's a much better path to choose. In fact, it's the only way to a happy existence.

It's the path I chose. How did that work out for me? You are going to love what happened. It was my reward for choosing the right response. I'm not talking about him wanting me back, although that day did come, but by then it was no longer what I wanted.

My ex told me the other woman didn't like that he and I didn't fight. She felt insecure and couldn't understand how we could be polite and kind to each other. That felt pretty damn good. But there's more. My cupcake got frosted, my friend. This is what he told her "Listen, if Keryl is a big enough person, after what happened to her, to not want to fight with me, I am not going to fight with her."

There you have it. *He defended me to her.* Do you have any idea how powerful and proud of myself I felt? Off the chain. One for the record books. Had I chosen to engage in a pissing contest, I would have felt small, weak, angry, and bitter. Who wants to feel that way?

You *always* have the choice in how to respond to what's happening in your life. It's our responses that shape us and affect our outcomes more than anything. Not the events themselves.

My ability to accept the situation as it was and choose an empowering response was largely due to my choice to forgive. This is how you rid yourself of emotional scar tissue—acceptance of a situation and letting go of the negative emotions that go along with it. *That's forgiveness.* That's power.

There are those who think some people don't deserve their forgiveness, and that by giving in, they will be perceived as weak. Let's explore this for a minute.

I'd be lying if I told you I wasn't pretty upset in the beginning. I hated his mistress without even knowing her. I resented her for stealing my husband. In fact, throughout the first few weeks, thoughts of her consumed me. She was all I could think about, and it was making me physically sick.

Let me ask you something. Who had power over how I felt? They did. Who was giving it to them? *I was.*

Nelson Mandela said *"Resentment is like drinking poison and hoping it will kill our enemy."* Think about how true that statement is.

We think we win by staying angry with people who've done us wrong. We think we are in a position of power. I've got news for you. Nothing could be farther from the truth. As long as we don't forgive, we're giving power over us to someone who doesn't deserve it. Screw that.

Look, we've all been screwed by someone at some point. Welcome to the club. If you really want to take your life back, then let go of it. Here's a way to do it.

Think about an event or actions of another person that still bothers you. Yes, sometimes, it's not a person we need to forgive; it's an event or situation. You may have one. You may have several. Take a minute now and write them down. Put each one on a separate piece of scrap paper.

Then what I want you to do is find at least one positive that came from each incident and write that on a pad of paper. Don't tell me there were no positive outcomes. I don't buy it.

For example, for me I would write on a scrap paper that my ex-husband had an affair. On the pad of paper, I would write that I am a much stronger and happier person and now enjoy an amazing relationship.

Once you identify a positive outcome, take the scrap of paper and do one of two things. Either tear it up in as many pieces as you so choose, or get up, walk over to the trash can and once and for all, throw it away. Better yet, step outside and burn it up until it disappears into thin air. Gone. Done.

You are deciding right now to forgive and release the power they've had over you, and all you are left with are your positives. You now own the power. You've forgiven and taken your life back. You are about to experience a newfound strength. I guarantee it.

Remember this. No one can hurt you without your permission. There is a major misconception about forgiveness. That it's for the benefit of the other person. Not necessarily. Here's what I believe. Forgiveness is for our benefit, not theirs. My forgiveness of my ex and his girlfriend was not for their benefit. *It was for mine.*

Every minute that you hang on to resentment and grudges, you are robbing yourself of a minute of happiness. This applies to the smallest of incidents: the person who cuts in front of you in line, or who cuts in front of you on the road. A happy bitch forgives, and she is infinitely more powerful and happier because of it.

Which brings us to another conversation on being powerful . . .

Baggage Drop

Lose this:

*Giving away power over your emotions
by hanging onto resentment and grudges of
other people and circumstances.*

Choose this:

Forgiveness. It is true power and sets you free.

5

◆

Your New Best Friend

Happiness is not a state to arrive at,
but a manner of traveling.
~Margaret Lee Runbeck

Have you ever climbed behind the wheel of a car, and as you put the car in drive and pressed on the gas pedal, you noticed something didn't feel right? Like there was some sort of resistance? Then you looked down and realized the emergency brake was on? I know I've done it. More times than I care to admit.

At first, you think *What the heck? Something's not right.*
Then you figure it out, hit the release and look around hoping no one noticed what a dumb-ass thing you just did.

I wonder what would happen if we didn't do anything
about the resistance. What if we just left it there, without
bothering to figure out the cause, and kept on driving? Getting to our destination would certainly take a lot longer. Plus,
we'd waste energy and cause unnecessary wear and tear on
our vehicle. My guess is eventually, we'd forget what traveling
smoothly even felt like.

Until the vehicle began wearing out, breaking down, and
demanding our attention and costly repairs. At that point,
we might question why. Even then, we would probably still
miss the root cause entirely, focusing on some external factors such as the car being a piece of shit, having too many
miles on it, or us just having crap luck. Sound familiar?

I wonder. Has life ever felt like that for you? As if tasks,
projects, work, home, relationships, *life in general* were more
difficult than they ought to be? Have you felt like some sort
of invisible force has been working against you? Are you
physically showing signs of wearing out and breaking down?
Do you suffer from headaches, fatigue, muscle aches, high
blood pressure, excess weight or anxiety? How about vari-
ous ailments that the doctors can't seem to tell you why the
symptoms exist?

Dr. Keryl at your service. *You're fucking stressed out, girlfriend!* Why? There is too much resistance in your life, and
your body is talking to you.

I know. No shit Sherlock, right? So, no surprise on the diagnosis, but the cause and treatment are going to surprise you. Especially since it doesn't require tests, pills or procedures. A cocktail once in a while with a girlfriend probably won't hurt, but even that isn't required. The treatment is simple. I'll explain in a minute. First, let's get to the bottom of what's causing the stress. It's probably not what you think.

If you're anything like me, you're a hard worker. I'm not at all afraid to work my ass off to get what I want. I don't have a problem with that. You probably don't either.

Except a while back, I went through a period of time when it seemed the more I busted my ass, the harder things got. Ever been there? For a while, I'd feel sorry for myself. Then I'd pick myself back up, grit my teeth, and give it another go, bound and determined to get results—only to get knocked down yet again as I came up short. Nothing I tried seemed to work.

On top of that, it seemed everywhere I turned, people around me had results and opportunities practically laid in their laps. *Son of a bitch! What am I doing wrong? What are they doing that I should be doing?* I knew damn well they weren't working as hard as I was. It wasn't fair. Life wasn't cutting *me* any breaks.

The truth is, it was beginning to piss me off. What's the deal? I'm smart. I'm a hustler. *This thing we call life shouldn't be this tough, should it?* It seemed the harder I pushed life, the harder it pushed back. Life was being a real bitch. Or so I thought.

Have you ever heard that one of the definitions of insanity is doing the same thing over and over and expecting different results? If that's true, I admit I was, at least temporarily, certifiably insane. I admit it. No two ways about it. My mind thought in order to get results, I needed to struggle, stress and work hard. Never mind that the more I did that, the less I accomplished.

Then, as we normally do only when we're at wits end, I started asking the right questions. Why did it feel like there was so much resistance in my life? Was life really this tough, or could it be me? If it was me, what did I need to do differently to get results easier, with less effort and fewer obstacles? Voila! I finally got the memo. I figured it out. Turns out life wasn't being such a bitch after all. I was. My own damn foot was on the brake.

The fact is, most of us have our foot on the brake. We don't have a clue that the reason life is so tough is *us*.

Believe me, I get that idea may be a little tough to accept. After all, if there is one desire we all share, it's for life to be easier, right? So why would any of us do anything to make life tougher? I'll tell you why. Because we haven't got a fucking clue we're doing it. That's why.

The cause, my friend, the diagnosis to our stressed life, is simply this: We are at odds with the present moment. Make no mistake. Life exists in one place and one place only. And that is right now—this very moment.

The problem is, many of us are living someplace else in our minds. We spend the bulk of our time either dwelling in the past or worrying about the future. Am I right? Except what change can come from that? I'll tell you what. Diddly squat.

What action can you take in the past? None. Unless you're a time traveler. Same goes for the future. This is the part that may be a little harder to wrap your head around. You believe you can take action in the future, but the fact is, when the future gets here, it is your new now. Past and future are mere thoughts in our heads. If that's where you live, life will continue to be a bitch. Why? No action can ever be taken in the past or in the future.

You see, life being a bitch has very little to do with your intelligence or luck. It has to do with your relationship with the present moment.

If you truly desire a more peaceful, relaxed, productive, and fulfilling life, you do that right now. Make room in your life for the present moment; she is about to become your new best friend.

Just as you would treat your best friend, you give her lots of attention, you accept her as she is, you trust her, and you certainly don't fight with her.

Treat her well, and she will do amazing things for you. No more wondering how others seem to have it so easy. *You* will be the one others look to, wondering how you can be so happy and relaxed and why results and good fortune come so easily to you.

Think back on one of the happiest and most relaxing moments of your life. I want you to remember where you were, who you were with, and what you were doing.

Let me ask you something. Where were your thoughts? Were they in the past or the future, or were they with you, completely and totally focused on the present moment?

They were with you, weren't they? Yes, they were. How do I know? It's the only place true peace and happiness exists. It's why vacations are so relaxing for us. Granted, the surroundings can be nice, but it's not the surroundings that affect our peace of mind as much as it is our ability to allow ourselves to be present. When your thoughts drift to the past or a future moment in time, you create a gap. That gap gives room for anxiety to creep in. The bigger the gap, the more anxiety.

What happens in our typical daily existence is we don't do that. We allow our thoughts to go off half-cocked, someplace else.

Take one of my closest girlfriends as an example. She is a gorgeous, top-notch professional, mom, wife, and friend. On the outside, her life appears to be in perfect order. All the pieces are in place. Except for one. She has a difficult time fully enjoying the moment she's in. Why? Because too often, her thoughts are somewhere else.

When she's on the phone closing a deal, she can't completely celebrate. Why? Her thoughts quickly drift away. Guilt over not spending more time with her family shows up and crashes the party. She hangs up the phone, shuts down the computer, goes to be with her family and guess what? Her thoughts are on work.

Don't we all do that? Have you ever been at work, thinking of what you need to do when you get home, and when you're home, you think about what needs to be done at work? Can you say *every freaking day?* Do you know what I call that? Nuts. That's what I call it. It creates stress. We're all guilty of it. How often you do it determines how much stress you will have in your life.

The anxiety comes from two fronts. First, not being relaxed right now, and second, we screw up, creating more problems, because we're not focused. Then what happens to the quality of whatever we are doing? It sucks balls, doesn't it?

Quality in anything requires care and attention. *Especially* as it applies to you as a person. Think of someone you consider to be a high-quality person. Does he or she have a high degree of presence? I guarantee it. You probably never put your finger on it before, but this is exactly why.

Let's explore this for a minute.

If you're at work, preoccupied and thinking about home, can you really be doing your best work? Conversely, if you're at home, stressing about work, are you being the best wife, sister, daughter, mother, friend you can be?

Think about it. Has your child or spouse ever asked you something, with you being well in ear-shot, but you didn't hear it? So he keeps repeating himself until it registers. By the time it does, you give him attention, except now you're annoyed by his badgering, and you snap. You're aggravated. He's aggravated. You're there, but you're not there. Your family senses it. Your relationships suffer.

How often have you caught yourself watching television, or in a conversation with someone and realize you just checked out? Have you ever read the same line in a book a half dozen times and not had it register? Do you misplace things? Think about how crazy that is. You physically had your keys in your hand. You set them down and yet were completely *unaware* you did it.

How much time do we waste searching for things we, ourselves put down? How about walking into a room and not remembering why you went there? How about driving somewhere and not remembering the entire trip? We chalk it up to having a bad memory, when it's simply lack of attention on the present moment. That's all it is.

So how do you fix it? It starts with raising your awareness. Instead of being wrapped up and controlled by your thoughts, you become the observer of your thoughts. The instant you catch your thoughts drifting away from right now and the task at hand, you become present.

Let me be clear here. I'm not suggesting you not look forward and plan. You have to. What I'm talking about is emotionally projecting yourself into the past or future, creating worry and *what if* or *I should be* scenarios.

You want quality relationships? You want to be your personal best? Wherever you are, whoever you are with and whatever it is you are doing, give 100 percent of your attention to that moment. There is peace and happiness in the simplest of circumstances. It's just that we're too wrapped up in traveling thoughts, we miss it.

Imagine going through life, with the same sense of peace as you do on vacation. That's the feeling you will experience when you give attention to the present moment. Try it out. See what happens. Take note of how you feel.

Care and attention are a big part of the deal. But there's more. Remember I said you need to treat the present moment as you would someone you care about, and how part of that involves trusting your friend and not fighting with her? When you do decide to give the present moment attention, it needs to be the right kind. Being angry at her or resentful of her isn't the sort of attention she needs. Give her that, and she will respond by throwing more challenges at you. That's a promise.

My friend, if you are not satisfied with your current situation right this second, you have two choices. Actually, three. We used to think there were only two. We'd say "Either change what you don't like or accept it." There's more.

One, you can stay in the situation and keep begrudging, resisting, and resenting it. You could continue to live every day easily aggravated, pissed off at the world for not making life easier and live as an angry, bitter, and unhealthy woman. Think about how that translates. *Maybe if I become angrier and more stressed, the universe will give me what I want.* For some of us, it's a thought pattern we learned at two years old, when our parents gave in to our temper tantrums. That's what I call being a bitcher and complainer, the kind I don't make room for. Their circumstances will head in one of two directions—stuck right smack where they are or get worse.

Your second option is you can trust that the present situation is there to serve you somehow, have faith that something good or better will come of it, and continue on as you were. Now the action you take is from a place of acceptance instead of resistance. Big difference in energy. Rather than getting up each morning, hating your job and feeling miserable before you even get there, you simply accept this is what you need to do for right now and make it the best it can be. Otherwise, you're only making the situation worse with self-created internal resistance.

Your third option is to again trust the present situation, accept it neutrally, without judgment or resistance, and take action to make changes from that state.

When our action and desire for change comes from a place of resenting the situation we are in, our outcomes are infected by that negative energy. I was pissed at life. I was resentful of other people. My actions and decisions were fueled by the wrong energy. What happened to my outcomes? They sucked. I thought it was my results and my outcomes that were causing me stress. It wasn't that at all. It was my *approach* to the tasks at hand that was the catalyst for everything.

Look at your own life. How much stress are you under? A fair amount, if you're like most people. Stress is an *epidemic* in today's society. Why? Because of backwards thinking. We think our stress is caused by our life circumstances, when, in fact, our circumstances are what they are because of our stressful approach to life. What's our stressful approach? Lack of present-moment awareness and creating unnecessary resistance to what is.

I can hear your *yeah buts* already. *Yeah, but I'm stressed because I don't have enough money. Yeah but, I'm stressed because I hate my job, my husband is lazy, there are not enough hours in the day.*

But *this*. Keep hating and resenting now, and you will continue to be unhappy. *It's why nothing has changed.* You've got a life partner, a best friend, the present moment, who will always serve you when you treat her well. When you are pissed at her, she's not going to do shit for you.

A while back, I participated in training in LA for a multi-million dollar company. The night before the training started, I had dinner with the owners. Our waiter, who was in his early twenties, was amazing. He thought of every little detail. You couldn't help but notice the care and attention he gave us. Right down to his checking on our meals.

"How awesome is everything?" he asked. Not "How is everything?" or "Is everything okay?"

Guess who was in the training the very next morning? The waiter. The owner hired him on the spot. That night, he was earning minimum wage. By the next morning, he was earning six figures. True story. That's the kind of shit that happens when you are highly present.

Most of us have convinced ourselves a host of other scenarios need to be in place before we can relax and enjoy life. When the reason none of these things are in place is because of how we treat the present moment. We've got it backwards. Read it again if you need to. I'm not being a smart ass. This is really important.

Girlfriend, far too many of us have reduced life to a means to an end. We're constantly just getting through this to get to that. We become so consumed by the goal, the end result, that we are resentful of what it takes to get there. We're doing whatever it is we're doing just to get it done. *It's why we're not seeing the results we want.*

We do it even with everyday tasks. We cook a meal in a rush to eat so we can move on to the next obligation. That's when we cut or burn ourselves. Not to mention, we are in a state of anxiety throughout the process. Do you clean or wash dishes just to get it over with? What have you dropped or broken? How about rushing through the grocery store with your thoughts on what you need to do when you get home only to feel stressed out the entire time and forget what you went there to get? Is that quality living?

What about searching for a new job and hating the process? Or wanting to find a partner and wishing you would just get the search over with? Look at the negative energy you are putting into the action. *The results we see are always a direct reflection of the energy behind the action to get there.*

Here's a new and better approach. Make your primary focus the enjoyment of doing. Even with the small stuff. It's what the young waiter did. Look what happened. Don't make your enjoyment dependent on a particular outcome. Think of your outcome as an invitation for things to work out nicely, instead of a demand. Put it out there as something you'd prefer, not something you *must* have.

Understand this. Our resistance to *what is* is much worse than the *what is* itself. Learn to be a little flexible. Become comfortable with a little unknown. That part was challenging for me. I wanted control. I wanted to plan everything out so there were no surprises. My divorce is a prime example. Was it part of my plan? No. Was I resisting it? Yes. Did I think I was getting a raw deal? Yes. Did it turn out to be the best thing that ever happened to me? Bet your ass it did.

Sometimes we have preconceived notions of exactly how we think life and events should play out. We like certainty, so we plan everything, believing so long as all goes as planned, we'll be happy. Well, guess what? It seldom does. When it doesn't, we think something's wrong. Then we create unnecessary resistance. We try to change that which isn't supposed to be changed. We jump into the ring, fighting with all we've got. And life bitch slaps us because we're fighting something we shouldn't.

We can still reach for our dreams and aspirations. There's nothing wrong with that. In fact, I encourage it. Just add a little of the secret ingredient: *focus on the present moment, and enjoy the process of getting there instead of delaying gratification or happiness until you arrive.*

Happiness isn't in the outcome. Happiness is in the doing. You will soon see when you choose to give attention to and take enjoyment in the present moment, suddenly, the outcomes will come to you, almost like magic. And they will come in greater abundance than you ever dreamed possible.

The same goes for the minor annoyances. Let me ask you something. How many times has your day not gone as planned? Do you get pissed off because of it? I know I have. I admit it. I used to see interruptions as some sort of invisible conspiracy out to make my life more difficult. There was no conspiracy. The problem was me. And the answer was entirely within my control.

I want you to imagine something. Suspend, just for a moment, any disbelief.

What if every single event, interruption or challenge that happens in your life is there for a reason that *benefits* you? What if every busted fingernail, run in your pantyhose, car that won't start, traffic jam, or husband having an affair, brought good to your life, or saved you from something much, much worse? How differently would you begin to see interruptions and changes in plans? How much more would you be able to enjoy every day, trusting and having faith, that it's all good? Imagine what that would do for your peace of mind and happiness.

One of my core beliefs is that everything around me is unfolding perfectly, and when change is happening, it is making room for something new, something better. All of us should live from that assumption.

Do I schedule and plan? Sure. It's a necessary part of life. But I also recognize that if something interrupts my plans, there is a greater reason. I accept that I may or may not ever get to see what it is, but I trust it is there. The universe often knows what we need better than we do. Sometimes it comes in the form of a bitter pill. It tastes like crap, and we sure as heck don't want it. But in the end, it does us a world of good.

We could spend a lifetime striving for and waiting for happiness by putting it dependent on circumstances outside of our control, events in the future, or in someone else's hands. *If only he would do this, then I'd be happy. If only I'd get that job, then I'd be happy. If only I could lose 10 pounds, then I'd be happy.*

I'll tell you what to lose. Lose the *if onlys*.

We're constantly just getting through so we can get someplace else or to some other situation and then be happy. Choose to live happily, or at least at peace with what is. Happiness isn't something you work towards; it's something you choose.

Making choices that bring me happiness is super high on my list of priorities, which leads us to . . .

Baggage Drop

Lose this:

Allowing your thoughts to continuously drift away from the present moment.

Choose this:

Live in the moment. Keep your thoughts and attention with you to live the best possible now you can.

6

◆

Happy is the *New Money*

*It's good to have money and the things
that money can buy, but it's good, too,
to check up once in a while and make sure that
you haven't lost the things that money can't buy.*
~George Horace Lorimer

Do you know the single biggest irony that lies at the root of all money problems? I'll tell you what it is in just a second.

First, let me ask you something. Outside of our very basic needs for survival, what each of us hopes to get, acquire, or do with money comes down to what?

How it will make us feel, right?

Whether we want more money so we can live in a nice apartment, get a bigger house, drive a newer car, dress well, travel, give to those we love, we're all after the same thing—a feeling. Call it sense of accomplishment, pride, satisfaction, whatever you want, but it all boils down to this: we believe it will make us feel happier.

Here's your irony: *The majority of us are somewhere between stressed out and downright fucking miserable in our quest to get that which will make us feel happy.*

Would you say that qualifies as ironic?

Maybe it's time we take a good look—I mean a really good look at what it is we're really after.

Aside from the very basic survival needs, what is your motivation for wanting more money? Are you after status? Maybe a sense of accomplishment? Do you want more material possessions and experiences? How about being able to give more to your family? What is it? Be honest with yourself.

At some point, every single reason I just mentioned has been a motivating factor behind my efforts. Maybe that's not the popular answer, but it is the truth. You know what else is the truth? *Not one of them* led to my sustained happiness.

Oddly enough, many of our reasons for striving for more money often lead us farther away, not closer, to what we really want.

We bust our asses, stress ourselves out, work in jobs we dislike, commute in traffic we despise, spend time away from our family to adorn ourselves, our children and our lives with expensive goods. Why? To impress others—to send a message that we are able to afford that which not everyone can. Some may disagree, but no one *needs* a BMW or a Mercedes. No one *needs* a $120 Ed Hardy t-shirt. No one *needs* diamonds and jewelry or designer shoes and purses. "Yeah, but they're the best quality." Really? Would these items still sell at the rate and price they do if the logos were stripped off? The answer is no, they wouldn't.

So let's play this one out. We sacrifice peace of mind, time to relax, time with family to be able to afford items that will do what? Impress others. Here's the kicker. Who are we trying to impress? Who are we attracting to our lives when we do this? *The type of people who will like or accept us because of what we have.* Then we wonder why we don't have sincere, high-quality relationships.

I'm not being critical. I'm trying to be helpful. The more we understand why we do what we do, the better equipped we are to do that which will truly make us happy. I've already told you I've had a host of differing motivations for having more money. I owned a BMW. I enjoy nice jewelry, clothes and shoes. I don't intend to stop buying these items. That hasn't changed.

What has changed is my willingness to give up that which is most important to me in exchange for having them. If I can indulge myself in the finer things in life and not trade too much time with those I love or my own peace of mind and happiness, terrific. But if owning material possessions means I will experience stress, anxiety or unhappiness, no thanks. I'd rather do without.

When are we really successful? When we can afford big houses and fancy cars? When we have a wardrobe to die for? If we infect our lives and the lives of those around us with anxiety and stress throughout the process of making money, how can we consider ourselves successful? If you're happy and enjoying life right now, you are successful today, right this very minute, regardless of how much money is in the bank or what kinds of cars are parked in the garage. Or, for that matter, whether or not you even have a garage.

Let's explore another, perhaps even more common mis-directed motivation for having more money.

We work too many hours in either an environment we don't care for, with people we dislike, or doing a job we don't like because *we want to provide a better life for our children.* On the surface, it seems honorable. So how is this misdirected?

If you are stressed out 40+ hours a week, physically and emotionally shot by the time you get home, what are your children learning from you? Fast forward to their adult life, and chances are, they will be living the very same reality you are today. If the manner in which you are living your life makes you unhappy, you are teaching your children by your actions that this is what you are supposed to do. How is that providing a better life for them?

On top of that, if you make it a habit to overindulge your children, what are you teaching them when it comes to them getting what they want? I'll tell you what. *Someone else will get it for me.* How is that going to play out for them as adults? Take a look at the behavior of many people who had so-called advantaged childhoods, and you'll have your answer.

As an adult looking back, I consider myself very fortunate to have grown up in a poor household. For the first few years of my life, I didn't even realize I was missing anything. I thought it was kind of cool that I got free lunches at school, and I was quite content to spend my summers playing Hide and Seek and Kick the Can, games, of course, that cost us nothing to play.

It wasn't until I hit junior high, where middle and upper class neighborhoods were combined with ours, that I realized there was something different. I discovered that other girls had their own bedrooms, went on vacations, and had bath towels so plush you could sleep on them.

Then I wanted more. Then the lessons began.

Soon after I started junior high, I fell in love. Not with a boy—with another girl's 10-speed bike. Never before had I wanted something so badly. I rushed home to tell my mother I wanted that bike. "You'll have to find a way to pay for it." she told me. "Your father and I can't afford it."

What kind of raw deal is this? Why couldn't my parents be like the other girls' parents? I'm not proud to say it, but the truth is I was pissed. I was convinced my life would be so much better if my parents could give me whatever I wanted.

Or would it? What happened as a result of their lack of money?

Not getting that bike wasn't an option. I simply wanted it too badly. Stealing certainly wasn't on the list of possibilities, and if my parents weren't going to buy it for me, how was I going to get it? That led to only one option. I had to figure out how to earn the money to buy it myself. What does a 13-year-old girl do when she wants to earn money? She baby-sits. A few months and my fair share of dirty diapers later, I became the proud owner of a brand spanking new 10-speed-bike.

This may seem like a relatively insignificant event from my childhood, but I believe otherwise. I believe this was one of the single-most defining moments of my life.

It is my earliest memory of knowing exactly what I wanted and having to figure out how I was going to get it. My mind learned to think not in terms of who would get something for me, but how I could figure out a way to make it happen. My parents couldn't afford to buy me expensive gifts, and that so-called limitation turned out to be the greatest gift they ever could have given me. As an adult, if there is something I want, I go get it. I figure it out. I don't sit back hoping or expecting for it to be given to me. Nor am I subjected to adult-onset temper tantrums when my sense of entitlement gets a rude awakening.

So I ask you, what do you want to hand your children? Money? Toys? Clothes? Cars? *Or the means and mindset to acquire them?*

If you're a mom, maybe a single mom, who is busting your ass day after day, feeling like a failure because of your inability to give your children what you never had, has it ever occurred to you that you have a distinct advantage? You have a ready-made opportunity to give your children something infinitely more meaningful and valuable—you and the lessons you can teach them—lessons that will serve them their entire lives. What more could you hope to accomplish as a parent?

I'm not suggesting any one of us give up on our quest to have more money. In fact, I'm a big advocate of being filthy-stinkin' rich. What I am suggesting is that we be careful what we potentially give up to get there. You think possessions, status, and experiences cost money? The real cost is our quality of life—today. We're leading ourselves into emotional bankruptcy.

We live a present moment of stress and unhappiness when we focus primarily on the end result. My friend, that *does not* get you closer to what you really want. The more you infect anxiety, worry and stress into the making of money, the harder it is to get, and the more you give up in exchange for it.

How about rather than focusing on what we will do with the money we make, we pay more attention to *how we go about acquiring it*. Why would this help us? For exactly this reason. Our motivation determines how we choose to approach earning money, and our approach dictates our outcomes.

Let's take a look at what a new approach would do for you if you never seem to consistently earn enough to live comfortably.

Week after week, there simply isn't enough money to pay the bills. Like some sort of emotional bladder infection, there is hardly a second of the day your mind doesn't worry about money. You have difficulty concentrating or enjoying anything you do, because wherever you go and whoever you are with, you can't escape the worry. You keep wishing something will change so you can at least keep up. That's all that's missing for you to be happy. Or so you think.

The problem here is your thoughts are consumed by all the wrong things. Get this next point and get it good. *The external set of circumstances in our lives is a direct reflection of the internal thoughts in our head.* Bottom line, you're carrying too much money baggage. Not money bags—money baggage. What's the baggage?

- Negative associations with money and wealth, including resenting those who have the very thing you want.
- Constant nagging worry about not enough money.
- A victim identity whose only wish is for the luck of a windfall.

Let's start with negative associations with money and wealth.

Any of these ring a bell? *Rich people are greedy. Money is the root of all evil. Money doesn't grow on trees.* Do you think if you heard these often enough from people who influenced you, that it might impact your ability to make money?

Bet your ass it does. It's baggage that's been handed to you, and it affects how you view wealth and your every action when it comes to money. People without money often have a stigma pegged to the wealthy, as if they must have stepped on or stole from others to gain their riches. What happens when you hold this belief? You end up with an internal tug of war. On one end of the rope, is the desire for more. On the other end, pulling in the opposite direction, is that part of you that believes having money isn't good.

Remember your driver? That part of you that directs your actions and behaviors? If you were handed the belief (the baggage) that rich people are greedy and money is the root of all evil, guess what? Despite your external, visible wants and conscious desires, your driver will sabotage your efforts. She's working against you. She will literally cause you to push money away from you. And you're not even aware it's happening.

Have you ever felt a bit like a boomerang? As if there are times you make a little progress and see the light at the end of the financial tunnel, only to have something snatch it away? That's not circumstance. That's your subconscious waging an internal conflict. It's confused.

I'll give you a perfect example. I own a rental property in an inner city. After a tenant had moved out, I was at the house, torn jeans, hair plastered with dirt and paint, cleaning disgusting kitchen grease and bathroom muck, working my ass off to get the home clean and decent for the next tenant. As I was upstairs putting knobs back on the doors, I heard a noise downstairs and went to investigate. A few steps down the stairs, I realized I had inadvertently left the front door open. About a half a second later, I spotted a knife someone had stuck into an interior door jamb. Yes, I said interior. Someone came into the house while I was upstairs working and left his calling card.

Now, let's look at what happened here. My BMW was parked in the driveway of an inner-city street populated primarily with people on the low end of the income scale. I had a few hundred dollars worth of tools on the first floor unattended. Whoever came in the house wasn't interested in stealing anything. He was interested in communicating with me. What was his message? "You are a rich person, and you don't belong here."

Whoever it was knew nothing about me. He had no idea the highlight of my return to school each year as a child was a new pair of shoes. Nor did he know that the reason I own that house was I invested the time, energy, risk, and thought to acquire that house and ten others without *any* of my own money.

My point is not to brag. My point is this: the knowledge and ability to create wealth is within me. Yet, this person literally pushed me away. Do you see my point?

Make no mistake here. Resentment of what others have repels money.

It's not only resentment that is a problem. Some of us have been led to believe that people change for the worse when they become rich. That's completely false. If you are a rich prick, I guarantee you were a prick first. Money doesn't make you a bad person. It simply shines a spotlight on your character, good or bad.

Look at what quality people like Oprah Winfrey or Bill and Melinda Gates are doing now that they are rich. They enrich the lives of millions of people with their generosity. *That's* what happens when good people become wealthy. They don't turn into bad people. Neither will you.

Be happy for the successes of others. Approach successful people with a sense of curiosity. Find out how they think, what they believe and do, what kinds of decisions they make. In doing so, you welcome and pull money closer to you—in a very literal sense.

Let's address the constant worry about lack of money.

Do you find yourself making statements like *I can never keep up, I never can get ahead,* or *Every time I get ahead, something happens to set me back?* This is something that you do not want to do on a regular basis. You will form beliefs. Beliefs upon which your driver acts.

Your worry becomes the mental force behind all your actions, decisions, and circumstances. They not only become instructions to your subconscious, but they also become broadcasts to the universe. What's going to happen? You will attract more worrisome situations.

"Yeah but, that doesn't change the fact that I don't have enough money to pay my bills."

Maybe not today it doesn't. But what about tomorrow? If the thoughts in our head affect and create our realities, today is the day to begin a new kind of thinking.

The first step for you is to choose to accept the situation as it is, right now, neutrally. You will take the most effective action from this place. I'm not saying you need to like it. Nor am I suggesting you stay where you are. Everything I am sharing with you is about getting you to a better place—either in your mind or in the reality of your circumstances, or of course, both.

Next, make it a habit to bring to mind, everything you are grateful for. Each time you catch yourself worrying, use that as a trigger to bring out feelings of gratitude. Then, the energy behind your decisions will be light years more effective and productive.

Finally, don't mentally label your situation. It could be a fact that you may need to turn in your car because you don't have enough income to keep it. That's neutral. That's a fact. When we turn that into a story such as *My finances are a disaster* or *I'm broke* or *I'm a failure,* our mental labeling and opinion of the facts amplifies our negative feelings and emotions about the situation. How effective then, will your actions be?

Now let's talk about the feelings of powerlessness, of feeling like a victim.

You could defend your poor financial state with a long list of reasons: *I got laid off due to no fault of my own, the economy sucks, my husband lost his job,* all which could be accurate statements. But let me ask you something. When your mind is focused on all the reasons you aren't in a better place, what action will you take to improve your situation? None. Why would you? You believe it isn't your fault. You are a victim.

Except the problem is that belief only perpetuates poverty and financial struggle. By belief, I mean, the attitude of resentment and that *cross my fingers, let's hope some miracle happens* and money comes pouring into your life. Hope sounds nice, but it's passive. It puts your financial future in the hands of fate, not in your own. Is that really where you want it?

If an unexpected event did happen, get over it. Mulling about how wronged you were won't help you. What do you need to do next?

You are not a victim. There is nothing wrong with you. You are not being punished. You do not deserve poverty and struggle. You are a deserving, intelligent individual. You're reading this book, aren't you? That in itself shows me you are ready to take charge of your life. So how do you do it? You start asking the right questions.

Start with this one. What would have to happen for me to live a superior life? What needs to be in place? This is a *huge* one. If the only question you ask regularly is *How am I going to get through next month?*, what are the answers you will get? The ones you have been getting. *How to just get by*. Do you want a lifetime of just getting by, or do you want a superior life?

Here's some more.
- What kinds of behaviors do I need?
- What action do I need to take?
- What do I love to do?
- What am I good at?
- How can I add value to the lives of others?

By the way, don't let me catch wind of you trying to make money at the expense of other people. A happy bitch would never do that. Always ask yourself how you can add value to the lives of other people. Take action on what answers come to that question and you will never run out of ideas to earn money.

You will surprise yourself with what answers come to you when you begin to ask the right questions.

Don't define who you are by your current set of circumstances. You are not a poor person. You are an intelligent, hard-working, fabulous female who is simply experiencing a temporary situation. You are a walking, talking, breathing miracle who is here for a reason.

Now let's talk about the person, maybe you, who is earning enough to live comfortably or even better than just comfortably, but you seriously dislike what you do or who you do it for. Your anxiety hangs around 24/7 like some sort of unwanted appendage. It follows you home every night, eats dinner with you, sleeps in your bed, and it's right there when you pour your first cup of coffee in the morning. You probably have trouble sleeping and barely have enough energy to get through the day.

You've built a lifestyle around the income your job provides and feel trapped. Your life is in a constant state of resistance because there is a huge gap between where you are and what you are doing and what you wish you could be doing.

Just like the person who is broke, the root of your problem lies with present-moment unhappiness. You feel the answer to your prayers would be to work somewhere else or not at all. *Then,* you will be happy. It's entirely possible you could legitimately be working in less-than desirable circumstances. I'm not here to dispute that. I'm here to help you make whatever changes needed to lead you to sustained happiness.

You have three choices. One, keep bitching and hating your situation. That is of course if you want to continue to be miserable. Two, accept where you are right now as neutral and lose the resistance, even go so far as deciding to enjoy the ride. Third, accept neutrally where you are, ask yourself empowering questions and start making changes.

If you are going to stay where you are, decide to kick ass doing it. You'll be amazed at what that one shift in perspective will do for you. Remember the story of the young waiter. What did kicking ass as a waiter do for him?

No matter what our challenges are with money, we all can benefit from an occasional self-check up. Let's take a step back and look at what it is we really want. What's most important to us? Is what we're doing and how we're doing it consistent with that?

We know what we set out to do, but sometimes we find ourselves in the midst of all the doing and unknowingly, we're chipping away at those very things in life we treasure most. Sometimes it happens in such tiny installments that we're not even aware it's happening.

The same with your body. No one really cares if they put on an extra half pound or pound of weight, do they? We don't even notice it. Except if we do that day after day, week after week, one day we look in the mirror and we're 25 or

50 pounds overweight. We stand there mortified, scratching our heads wondering how the fuck we got that way. I'll tell you how. One bite at a time. It didn't come from eating one massive meal. It came from thousands of little choices that added up to 25 or 50 pounds. Same with making money.

We make statements like *As long as you have your health, you have everything* or *I wouldn't trade my family for all the money in the world.* I believe we mean what we say at the time we say it. I know I do. Except I continue to see smart and loving women, myself included, chip away little by little, at the priceless treasures we say we'd never trade.

There are times I catch myself making one more phone call, sending one more e-mail, or completing one more little task that I can cross off my list after my husband asks me to sit and spend time with him. He can wait another two minutes, can't he? He'll be fine. Or will he? Am I not trading little bits of him when I do that?

It isn't necessarily the major life decisions that affect us as much as the daily, seemingly insignificant choices that add up over time. It's not the one French fry or the one piece of chocolate that's the problem. It's the accumulation of the *one mores* that are the problem. It's when the *one mores* becomes a way of living. How many times can I say to my husband "One more e-mail and I'll be right there!" before he begins to feel like there's always something a little more important?

Will there be days or even weeks at a time where we are pushing toward a goal or busier with the business side of our lives than usual? Yes, of course. Is that okay? Yes. Absolutely.

Let's just not let that become our norm. Let our actions on the outside reflect what's most important to us on the inside.

Think of it this way. Remember when we were kids and were fascinated by the idea of treasure maps? The prospect of stumbling upon a cryptic piece of paper having the capacity to take us to a buried treasure was captivating.

Imagine for a minute that treasure maps really do exist, and today you stumbled upon two maps and had to choose only one. The first is guaranteed to lead you to $5,000,000. The catch is the route could involve struggle, worry, stress, and an undetermined amount of time away from people you care about. It might even involve illness or injury.

The second map has a different sort of guarantee. You are certain to experience a fun, exciting and fulfilling journey. The catch with this map is although it could lead you to the treasure, it wouldn't be guaranteed.

Which of the two would you choose?

At first glance, most of us would choose the second map. I mean, who the heck would consciously choose to put a price on their peace of mind or health?

In fact, everyone I've ever asked this question of say they would choose the map of fun and relaxation. The irony is, that's not how most of us are living. As a matter of fact, many of us are living in direct opposition to the choice we think we'd make. How are you living now? There's the real answer. We're selling our peace of mind and health for our own personal treasures. This is precisely how we get off track. *If I suck it up now, it will pay off later.* Sound familiar? Except we end up sucking it up year after year after year. We're focused on the goal, on the big win, the payoff down the road. The answer doesn't lie in the destination. The answer lies in the method of getting there. Let's make it about the ride.

It wasn't until I very deliberately chose meaning and enjoyment of the doing versus the outcome that I really became happy making money. Leave your existing motivations in place. I'm not telling you to completely get rid of them. I haven't. I'm just suggesting you adjust the order a little. Bring enjoyment of doing and living to the very top of your priorities.

Choose to be happy now, regardless of whether you have all the money you desire. If you put off your happiness until the money arrives, you may discover money wasn't the magic wand you thought it would be.

If money truly answered all prayers and brought happiness, why do we see millionaire entertainers and heiresses to great fortunes spiraling out of control, in and out of rehab and even committing suicide because life is so unbearably unhappy?

Is it wrong to want money? Is that the problem? No and no.

Wanting money is healthy. More of us should freely strive for it. The truth is, I would *love* for you to go out and make sick amounts of money, have a ball doing it, and thoroughly enjoy the freedoms money can provide. I want you to have it all. Not pieces of success. All of it—money, health, love, and happiness.

Make happy the new money, and you'll be rich beyond your wildest expectations.

Don't worry about making the perfect decision every single time. You won't. It's okay. It's about a sense of awareness to balance accomplishment and money with spending quality time with those we love, without sacrificing our own peace of mind, which brings us to . . .

Baggage Drop

Lose This:

Sacrificing peace of mind and happiness for money.

Choose This:

Put happiness into your efforts to earn money.

7

---◆---

Do What Makes You Happy

By plucking her petals, you do not
gather the beauty of the flower.
~Rabindrath Tagore

Have you ever noticed that there are life lessons happening all around us? Sometimes they pop up in the most unexpected places—even airplanes.

In the midst of performing the ever so elegant left-to-right ass shift while simultaneously shoving my pocket book underneath the seat in front of me with my foot, there it was. My next life lesson. Who was my teacher? The flight attendant.

As she went through the safety instructions, it occurred to me that perhaps at least every once in a while, I ought to pay attention. Maybe I had just read about a plane crash. Who knows? For whatever reason, I decided to take a dose of my own medicine, become present and give her my attention.

"In the unlikely event of sudden loss of cabin pressure, oxygen masks will drop from the compartment over your head." she advised. She went on to tell us how to put the mask on properly and told us to breathe normally. Breathe normally? Yeah, right. My lungs would be sucking in air like a freaking shop vac if we lost cabin pressure. Anyway, here's my point. What does she tell us to do if we are traveling with a small child?

She tells us to put our own mask on first. The reason is pretty obvious. *Because if you don't take care of yourself first, you're useless to the child.*

Perfectly understandable. We don't view it as selfish to take care of ourselves first. It's a simple matter of common sense. Well, at least it is when we're sitting in 23A. By the time we're half-way to baggage claim, we've left our common sense behind.

How so? How did the harebrained idea ever get started that being a good woman means you put the needs of your family first in every instance? It's one of the most widely held beliefs among women. However, it doesn't necessarily mean the most common beliefs are the most accurate ones. The vast majority of women also believe bitching at her man will motivate him to do as she wants. Hmm, wonder how that's been going.

Back to my point. You may be inclined to disagree with me. You could take the position that you experience joy when you do for your family. If that's truly the case, if you really feel better, happier, more relaxed and fulfilled when you do for them, cool deal, you've got it figured out. Bringing joy to others, in my book (and this literally is my book) is essential to living happily. But not when that belief results in you being drained of life, energy and happiness. Which is exactly what happens when we take this principle to extremes.

What are extremes? When we bury our wants and desires so deeply under an oppressive pile of "necessaries" and "shoulds" that we forget what happy even feels like.

We build a life where we exist solely for the purpose of someone else. We toss aside any thoughts of what we want and feel guilty about doing what would make us happy.

I refuse to believe that is how we are supposed to live as women.

We give up on expressing our thoughts or fantasies through the book we've always wanted to write, taking piano lessons, or going to Italy. We even cast away our little wishes like taking a quiet bubble bath, watching our favorite show (in our sweat pants with hair up, of course) without interruptions or curling up with a good book and a glass of wine.

Instead, we get up and go, react to the next demand with not so much as a flicker of a pause to question what would make *us* happy.

Think for a minute how this translates. "I'll do what everyone around me wants, even if it makes me miserable doing it. That's just how it is." After all, we're women, right? We're supposed to live a life of sacrifice for those we love.

Or are we?

Come on. You and I are smarter and more deserving than that.

Continually sacrificing your own happiness for someone else's may be a family recipe handed down from generation to generation, but all it's cooking up is depression, anxiety and resentment. Here's the kicker. You and your family are dining on the same damn dish.

I'm not remotely suggesting life becomes all about you. Not at all. What I am suggesting is it becomes even just a little more about you. I want you to dig out from underneath the pile of demands and find a better balance. One that is better for you *and* those you love. How do you go about doing that?

Let's start by establishing some common ground.

Unless you're a complete bitch, which I highly doubt, you and I (and every other female for that matter) share a few desires.

1. You want to live a happy life. I know that's the case for two reasons. One, you're reading this book. And two, who doesn't? I mean, why else are we on this ride?

2. You want those you love to live a happy life.

3. You want to contribute to the happiness of those around you.

All true, right?

So here's what I wonder. Are any of these more important than the others? Are they in conflict with each other, and are we supposed to choose among them? Or can we have it all?

I'll take door number three, please. I want it all. Don't you?

Our expectation and belief is that when we are thoughtful of others, they will be happy and in turn, so will we. That basic premise is dead nuts on. I don't doubt that we set out with the best of intentions.

Except here's where we have the tendency to get off track. Our effort to make those we love happy begins to feel just like that—an effort. It turns into a sacrifice.

Make a mental note. What we do for those we love, with the intention of contributing to their happiness, should *also* contribute to our own.

The energy we put into our actions affects and infects our outcomes. If you feel you are making a sacrifice for someone you care about and feel a sense of disappointment in what you are giving up, you've just added to your own unhappiness. Despite how it may appear on the surface, you have not contributed to the long-term happiness of the other person. Trust me. You haven't. If you're unhappy, don't you think they sense that? Don't you think what you feel rubs off on them?

The more you do what makes you unhappy, you perpetuate more unhappiness all around you. You're brewing a big pot of resentment stew. You keep it on a slow simmer, adding more and more into the mix, until one day, it boils over, and you burst.

"I've given up so much for you, and you've never appreciated it! Is this the thanks I get?"

Turn it around for a second. If your husband did something nice for you, and you knew it left him feeling like he missed out, would you feel happy about receiving? How could you? But when you know he feels joy through what he does for you, how do you feel? Happy. So does he.

Both your happiness and the happiness of those around you can and should be achieved simultaneously. There really is no other way. One doesn't take the place of the other. One *feeds* the other. *Your happiness contributes to theirs.* It doesn't take away.

Earlier in the chapter, we agreed on some common desires, one of which, was our desire to contribute to the happiness of those we love. Doing that which makes you happy is part of how we do that. If your friends, family, spouse, especially your children, know that you place importance on your own desires, what's going to happen?

Two things. One, by learning from you, they too will make their own happiness a priority. Isn't that what you want for them? And two, they will be more aware of and focused on your happiness. If those around you seem to hardly care what you want, think about why that is. I'll tell you why. *They learned it from you.* They are placing the same amount of importance on your happiness that you do.

My first husband didn't go out of his way to think about what I wanted. Why would he? I taught him by my actions that my wants were unimportant. Where do you think I learned that?

Back in my kick-ball days, it was normal for my mother to wait on my father hand and foot. By that, I mean getting up every single day at dawn to pack his lunch, have dinner ready the minute he walked in the door, and tiptoe around the house, warning three energetic young girls to do the impossible—be perfectly quiet as to not wake him up from his nap. His wants and needs trumped hers. Every time. What did that get her? The same thing it got me.

Remember the story of me finding my mother sobbing at the kitchen table after discovering my father's affair? Fast forward 25 years as I sat at my own kitchen table sobbing on the phone to my sister for the same damn reason.

My brain set out on a search and rescue mission, pulling up every past memory, analyzing my every move for what I could have done to have been a better wife. *There must be something I missed.* Oh, I missed something all right, but it wasn't what I thought.

My pathetic little self waited on my ex hand and foot. You may think I'm exaggerating. I'm embarrassed to say I'm not. After downing the last of his bourbon Manhattans, he'd reach his glass in front of me without saying a word and shake the ice cubes. Guess whose sorry little ass got up and made him another one?

Annoyed at my arriving home a few minutes later than usual one night, he sat at the kitchen table, waiting for dinner, with a clear expression of annoyance on his face. Keryl of today would have told him to kiss her happy bitch ass and make his own dinner. Keryl of yesterday kept her timid mouth shut, made and ate dinner in silence, cleaned up and cooked the next night's dinner that evening. I dished it out, wrapped the plates in plastic and stuck them in the fridge so I'd need only a few minutes in the microwave the next day. As I said, I'm not exaggerating. I acted like his servant.

I've got to tell you. I don't blame my ex for having an affair. I really don't. I mean, who really wants a pathetic spineless woman following them around? Does any worthwhile man really want that?

Let's look at the underlying belief and the twisted way this plays out. *If I put my needs and wants aside and care only about what makes him happy and what he wants, I will make him happy. If I make him happy, I've been a good wife, and I'll feel good.*

Except what happened instead? He's unhappy and goes on the prowl. I'm miserable, crying at the kitchen table. In a mirror-like fashion, my role as a wife played out exactly like my mother's.

I believed that living in sacrifice would make him happy and would make me a good woman. I accomplished neither.

I heard it said once that the best way to help the poor is not to be one of them. I've come to believe that the same philosophy applies to happiness.

By constantly sacrificing what we want, we're living a life less than we were meant for. We are intelligent, loving and magnificently creative women. Our job is not to give up on everything we want, for fear of being selfish. *Our job is to live happily* and by doing so, we help those around us do the same.

A happy bitch treats others *and herself* as she wants to be treated. Do unto others is a great moral compass. So is do unto yourself.

How do we start doing that? We just took the first and most important step—understanding why we need to place our desires higher up the priority chain.

As I recovered from my divorce, I wanted to understand why it happened, and what I could have done differently. It sure as hell wasn't more of the same pussy-footing around I'd done for eleven years.

I needed to figure out what changes and adjustments I had to make to *me* to make my second time around a heck of a lot better. Yes, I said to *me*. We'll put ourselves in the nut house if we keep trying to change circumstances outside of our control. Here's the revelation: in order for things to change, we must change. Who has complete and total power to do that? *We do.*

What were the first changes I made? I started caring about what *I* wanted. It may have taken me 25-plus years, but I finally figured out something about men. They want to know you want them and that they are important to you, but they'll be bored stiff if there is no challenge to you whatsoever. If you constantly cater to them without regard for your own happiness, in their minds, they have conquered you. Exit excitement, intrigue, and happiness. Enter boredom, dissatisfaction, and unhappiness—for both of you. Throw another carrot in your misery stew.

Start by getting in touch with what *you* want—with what makes you happy. That may even feel awkward for you at first. It did for me. Shortly after I left my ex, a counselor told me "You need to take time for you. Do what makes you happy." I left her office scratching my head and confused as all get out, because the truth is, *I couldn't think of anything.* I'm not kidding you. I didn't have a fucking clue what would make me happy. The concept was foreign to me. I had pushed my happiness aside for so long that I had forgotten what it felt like.

As I continued to give it thought, I figured out I liked watching whatever show I wanted to when I wanted to, or going to the mall and staying there just as long as I felt like it. I had fun going out dancing with my girlfriends, going to dinner with them, acting like a complete ass, and not caring who thought what. After a while, I got pretty damn good at this "What do I like?" game.

As a matter of fact, I've become quite the pro at it. I'm very in touch with what makes me happy. I pay very close attention to my gut, my instinct, how I feel vs. what I think. Happiness is a huge priority for me, and I make very deliberate decisions with that in mind. What do you think that has brought into my life as a result?

Life with my husband is amazing. He puts my happiness very high up on his list of priorities. Why? Because *I* do. Can you see how this works?

Now, I'm not suggesting you turn into a bitch and take on an attitude of "Screw you! It's my turn." I am suggesting you start by asking yourself "What would make me happy here?" If this is new for you, start with the little things. If someone asks you where you want to go for dinner, don't say "I don't care." Start caring. Start having a mind and heart of your own.

You can take this same theory and apply it to your life if you are a parent. Do you feel as if your children don't appreciate you? Could it be because you bend over backwards, run them here and there, buy them this and that, without taking time for yourself? It's a modern-day parent trap. Your children are learning by your every behavior. Will they believe you if you tell them their happiness is important, as you scrap your own? Is that really preparing them to go on and live their own happy lives? Chances are, they will go on to live their adult lives in very much the same way you have.

What better case can I make for you, right now, to begin living the sort of life you want them to live?

What I want you to take away from this chapter is this. Be careful about putting yourself into the absolute trap—where you try to be everything to everybody all the time. It's impossible. You're setting yourself up for heartache and stress. Find the balance. Be thoughtful of those you love. There's nothing wrong with that. It's natural for us as women, but do for you too. Do what makes you happy. You deserve it. They deserve it.

When you make your own happiness a priority, those who truly love you will respect you and love you even more for it, which brings us to . . .

Baggage Drop

Lose this:

Trying to please others at the expense of your own happiness. Feeling guilty about doing for yourself.

Choose this:

Make your happiness important. Do what makes you happy, and your happiness will spread to those around you.

8

◆

*How we spend our days is, of course,
how we spend our lives.*
~Annie Dillard, The Writing Life

Have you ever picked up a newspaper and read about someone who committed suicide? What were the first thoughts
that came to you? How sad it was that another human being chose to end her life? Her head must have been pretty
messed up. Certainly, no one in her right mind would end
her life early. Or would she?

The sad reality is millions of people in their so-called "right mind" are doing just that every day. Maybe not as quickly as the person who puts a gun to his head or jumps off a bridge, but they are.

Look at the leading causes of death in the United States—heart disease, diabetes, and cancer. If you're under the impression that whether or not you suffer from these diseases is based only on family history and bad luck, think again. Many are due to lifestyle choices.

What does that mean to you in plain English? The biggest factor in whether or not you get these diseases, is you.

If you want to live a happy life, you need to make sure the *life* part is there.

By the way, I am not a nutritionist or a personal trainer. I'm just a happy bitch who is going to share some little nuggets of insight that have worked for me.

Let me start by asking you something. When I say to you "healthy lifestyle," what comes to your mind? If you're like most people, you think diet and exercise. What if I told you that's only half correct? You see, there is an often overlooked but just as critical component—the health of your mind.

Is it not common knowledge that excessive anxiety can make us sick or even kill us? Yes. Why? Because our mental state affects our physical state, right? Same goes for the reverse. If we eat crap food, don't exercise, and end up overweight or obese, drunk and smoking, what does that do for our minds? There are women who cry *every day* because they hate how they feel and look. They're embarrassed to shop for clothes, go swimming in the summer, or even have their pictures taken.

Mind and body are inseparable. When we choose to take better care of our health, we have to consider both.

The good news is it's not that complicated. There are only four elements you need to consider: what you consume, exercise, rest, and treats.

Let's begin with what you consume. You've heard since you were five years old that you are what you eat. Have you ever seen the commercial with the girl walking away from the camera with cinnamon buns stuck to her ass? That's us, girlfriend. What we eat absolutely affects how our bodies look and feel. And who gets to choose what we eat?

I realize you understand this already. Except I want to point out a not-so-subtle distinction when it comes to the effect of food on our bodies. It isn't the fat, calories, or volume of food we eat that makes us overweight. It's our *choice* to eat the food that makes us overweight.

Think of it this way. If you run two miles and sweat, did the running cause you to sweat? Sort of. More directly, it was your *choice* to go running that did. See the difference? The problem isn't the food. The problem, or rather where the solution lies, is in your choice whether or not to eat the food.

Don't give food that much power over you. Are you going to let a cheeseburger and French fries determine your happiness? Screw that!

I'm not going to go into detail here on what you should or should not eat. There are tons of resources out there for that. The fact is, you already know what's good for you and what's not. It's not a question of what. The million-dollar question is *How do we get ourselves to do what we know we need to do?* I'm going to show you how in just a moment.

Before I do, let's talk about what your mind consumes. You already know that if you eat shit foods, your body is going to look and feel like shit. Well, guess what? If you feed your mind crap, what do you think your life is going to look like? Garbage in, garbage out. If you look around at the circumstances in your life right now and don't like what you see, the answer is to feed yourself healthier mind food. Plain and simple.

Women surround themselves with negative people who bitch about other people and their lives, watch reality TV and the news, and all they read are the rags. Then they scratch their crap-filled heads wondering why they can't seem to get a break. *Hello!*

Pay close attention here. I've said it before. *The circumstances in our lives are a direct result of the thoughts in our heads.* You want to transform your body? Take better care of it. You want to transform your life circumstances? Take better care of your mind. It starts with what you feed it.

So what constitutes a healthy mental diet?

They tell us breakfast is the most important meal of the day because it gets our energy going, right? The first meal you eat (or skip) sets the physical barometer for your day. So let me ask you something? What's the first *food* you give your mind each morning? Do you sleep until the last possible second, then rush around, stabbing your manicured nail through your pantyhose, burn your head with the curling iron, or worse, go to work with a bad hair day because you didn't have enough time to get it right? Seriously, what kind of intellectual and emotional tone are you setting for yourself? You might as well climb back in bed. And guess what? Sometimes we do.

What are you feeding your mind at the beginning of each day? If it's the news, think twice. News is negative. News is what is wrong. You're setting your life's radar detector to look for what's wrong with the world. I'm not telling you not to stay in touch with what's happening, but is that really how you want your day to begin? Stay in touch, that's fine, but if news is all you watch or read, you will be fooled into believing that we live in a sad world filled with horrible people. You will believe that the majority of people are thieves, child molesters, wife beaters, and murderers. Are there bad people out there? Yes. But every day, in every moment, miracles are happening and opportunities are presenting themselves *right in front of us*. The problem is, we're not on the lookout for them.

Have you ever thought about buying a new car? What happens as soon as you decide what make, model and color you want? The exact car you picked out starts popping up everywhere. Did the rest of the world get the memo that you are buying a new car and decide to copy you? Of course not. There aren't any more of that exact car on the road since you made your decision. The only difference is your level of awareness.

Back to TV. News isn't the only source of negativity on television. Do you realize that many of us let people into our homes, through our televisions, that we would never allow in the front door? Something is seriously wrong with that.

I'm not knocking television completely. If you learn, grow, laugh, and feel happier or more relaxed by what you watch, go for it. But the vast majority of what is on television is deliberately negative and dramatic. It's what sells. Producers of reality shows intentionally select volatile, controversial, adversarial personalities to be on their shows. Watching these types of people interact, not to mention their nauseating disrespect for themselves and other people, would have you believing those are the kinds of relationships to expect in life. What you see is what you get, my friend. Is that what you want? Then why spend your precious time feeding on it?

Plus, it doesn't end when the show is over. You go to work or hang out with your friends and relive it. You talk about what a jerk so and so is, and you couldn't believe what that bitchy real housewife did, what a drama queen she is, blah, blah, blah. The more you talk about it and experience it, the more garbage you are feeding your brain.

I can tell within just a few minutes of talking to someone what their mental diet consists of. It sticks out like an oversized ass in two-sizes-too-small spandex. There's no missing it. I can tell by what people talk about, the stories they tell, their perspectives and most of all, what they complain about.

Case in point. My parents were over for dinner a few weeks ago. My dad is semi-retired and works as a handyman doing minor repairs for a couple of local landlords. Within a few minutes of arriving, my dad said, "What a shitty day I had today." He went on to tell us about the asshole tenants in the buildings, how they are rude and live like pigs. He was even mimicking one of them complaining.

What does my father feed his mind? He reads the newspaper every day. He adjusts his day in order to get home in time to watch Jerry Springer. I'm serious. I'm not making this up. He says it amuses him. What does that show consist of? Drama, losers, uncontrolled outbursts of anger, slamming other people, and on and on and on.

What has my father trained his brain to notice and see in others?

I'm not picking on him. It's simply how it is. It is a fact that our lives will manifest for us precisely what we focus our attention on. What do you want in your life? Feed yourself more of what you want, not what you don't.

I begin every day by reading for a minimum of 15 minutes. I'm not talking about romance novels, which I enjoy too. I save that for down time. I'm talking about books that inspire me emotionally or teach me intellectually. By reading in the morning, I am setting the tone of expansion, of growth, for my day, and ultimately my life. You may have demands that may make morning reading a challenge. So choose a time of day that works for you. Set aside at least 15 minutes a day to read something that makes you feel good inside, increases your expectations of life, restores your hope or grows your mind.

How committed are you to living a happier life? If you're not willing to do that, you have no right to complain about the state of your life. You really don't. As a matter of fact, how about taking that time you used to spend complaining and use it to learn?

Don't kid yourself. Your seemingly insignificant daily habits aren't so insignificant.

Watching television and reading books aren't our only sources of mind food. What about the people with whom we surround ourselves? Do you think the attitudes, beliefs, and emotional state of the people around you affect yours? How can they not?

I am very selective about who I spend time with. I make no bones about it or apologies for it. If you are a downer, and someone who regularly focuses on what's wrong instead of what's right, if you like to talk negatively about other people and situations on a regular basis, blame other people for the state of your life or are selfish, I ain't hanging around you. It's that simple.

One of my core beliefs is that relationships shouldn't be work. So guess what my life manifests for me? Awesome relationships. I have people in my life who go out of their way to support me, help me fulfill my dreams, who are fun and empowering. *That is by choice and by design.*

It doesn't mean each of us doesn't have bad days. We all do. If a friend is momentarily down and needs to vent, I let her. What I'm talking about is when every day is a bad day by the perspectives people choose to take.

Start paying attention to the poor mental habits people have, the effect it has on their lives, and subsequently yours. It's up to you to decide if that's what you want. I'd rather be alone with my own thoughts I get to control than be around other people with negative thoughts and beliefs. Any day.

Should you ditch long-time friends or family members for that matter if they have a habit of negative thinking and living? Not necessarily. You can help influence them positively by your behavior and the better choices you are making. Take the lead. Set the example. People in my life know I'm not going to engage in negative conversations. They just don't go there.

If you choose to approach the topic with them, make sure it comes from a place of caring and a genuine desire to help, or don't say anything at all. If they don't get it after a while, then you have a decision to make. Perhaps you don't drop them from your life altogether, but you can choose to limit how much time you spend with them.

Bottom line, choose your mental diet carefully—what you watch and read, the people with whom you surround yourself, and the types of conversations in which you engage.

Now let's talk about exercise.

Again, there are people a heck of a lot more qualified than I am to educate you on fitness. What I can do for you is help you understand why it's been challenging for you in the past to stick to an exercise routine. I'll also show you what to do about it. First, I want to raise an important question.

Why do we view exercise in this society as a luxury? Seriously. I work out on a regular basis. Someone said to me recently, "Must be nice to be able to go to the gym." You know what? Kiss my skinny ass! It's not a luxury. Does it help us look better? Yes. But that's not all it's about. Looking good is a pleasant by-product. Exercising reduces our risk of cancer, heart disease, stroke, injury, and extends our life expectancy and quality of life. It even helps us think more clearly. Luxury? No. I call it living.

Let's face it, girlfriend, exercising does help us look better. Then what happens? We have more confidence and feel better about ourselves. Who benefits from that? Everyone around us, including us.

You already get all this. The question is, how do you get yourself to follow through on an exercise routine?

Have you ever made a declaration to yourself that you were going to start exercising and get in shape? Maybe even as a New Year's resolution? What happened? If you're like 98% of the population, you started with great intentions and then didn't keep up with it. Want to know why?

Because your subconscious (your driver) knows you haven't kept your word in the past, so she doesn't believe you.

You make statements like *I am going to lose 20 pounds, I'm going to work out three days a week, I'm going to cut out the sweets*. What does your subconscious say? *Yeah right. We've been through this before. I don't believe you*. What happens then is there is a part of you sabotaging your resolutions before you even get started.

So all you need to do is prove to your subconscious that you mean business. Give her new data to draw from. Watch how easy this is.

Here's what I want you to do. Pick one small activity you can do in support of your exercise goals that is *super easy*. I mean like, any-moron-can-do easy. What is one bit of physical activity you can do every day, no matter how you feel or what the weather is like? Could you jog 30 steps or even just 15, do eight sit-ups or pushups every day, no matter how busy you were or how you felt? If your decision is to eat healthier, could you leave one bite of food on your plate at each meal, drink an extra glass of water each day or eat one piece of fruit a day? Of course you could. Pick something ridiculously simple.

Then do that one activity for 21 days in a row. Remember, that's all it takes to form a new habit. Just imagine, in three weeks' time, you will have proven to yourself (actually, to your subconscious) that you are a person who makes healthier choices. Then guess what happens? You will have handed over new instructions to your driver. Then, you'll be operating on virtual auto-pilot. Keeping up on exercise and healthy food choices won't require conscious effort. This is exactly what you want . . . healthier habits that no longer feel like a sacrifice or struggle. Imagine that.

I even created a chart for you to use to keep track. Go to my website www.HappyBitchBook.com and you can download it free.

By the way, don't put too much pressure on yourself to be perfect. None of us are. It's all right. If you miss a day, just pick up the next day and keep at it.

Don't believe me? Prove it to yourself. What do you have to lose (other than a few pounds)? Do this just one time, with one change, and watch what happens. After that, you can choose to adjust *any* unwanted behavior following the same format.

One final thought on physical exercise. Don't let it be something you fit in when you get everything else done. Make it a priority. Make an appointment with yourself to exercise, and keep it!

Let's look at the other piece of the exercise puzzle. We're talking about your mind and body. It's common knowledge that if we are sedentary, our muscles atrophy. They actually shrink. Well, guess what? *So do our minds.*

My grandmother lived until 95. Her brother lived until 99. They were both relatively sharp later in life. My uncle could change out a hot-water heater, send e-mails and discuss the stock market with my husband until his late 90s. Why? He never stopped exercising his mind. Both he and my grandmother did word-search puzzles, played cards, watched shows that taught them something. If you asked them how they lived so long and well, they would both tell you keeping your mind active is key.

Learning doesn't end when we graduate. Not even close. Your mind has an amazing capacity to learn, grow and create. It's a complete waste of the most powerful resource you have to not utilize it. Jim Rohn said, "Formal education will earn you a living; self-education will earn you a fortune." I believe it.

I know people who turn the television on as soon as they wake up in the morning, and it stays on all day long, even when they aren't paying attention to it—even when they're not in the room. It becomes like some sort of background filler. It's the brain's equivalent to being a couch potato. It's allowing your mind to be lazy. Rather than exercising it with self-generated, creative thoughts, you rely on an external source to feed you shit to think about. And it usually is just that, shit.

Are there times when you just want to veg out and not think too hard? Yes. Me too. That's totally cool. There are times we need that. However, also make a conscious effort to read and learn. Watch shows and talk to people who expand your mind. It will pay off more than you can imagine in the quality of your life and level of happiness.

We talked about consumption and exercise. Let's now talk about the third element, rest. With all the good physical exercise does for you, is it possible to go to extremes? Sure is. Think about it. What would happen if you decided you wanted to run from where you are to a town 100 miles away? Now, it may take you a few weeks, but most of us could do it. But not without what? Periods of rest, right? When our body feels tired, we know we need to take a break and give ourselves a chance to regenerate.

Well guess what most of us fail to do? Rest our minds. Think about it. If we ran and ran and ran without taking a break, our body would eventually give out on us, right? It would break down. Doesn't it make perfect sense that our minds operate *exactly* the same way?

When our brains are constantly flooded with endless thoughts, questions, and worries, we become mentally exhausted. If it goes on for too long, and we don't cut ourselves some slack, what happens? Our minds break down. We become overwhelmed and shut down. This, my friend, is what you call a nervous breakdown. Look at the life of today's typical woman. Is it really any wonder why so many people suffer from anxiety and depression?

We need to learn to slow our thoughts down and rest our over-active brains. Anxiety is our mind's way of telling us to take a break, that it needs a rest. We need to listen to it.

So how do we give our minds a break? I'll give you two suggestions. The first is to become aware of your thoughts, not only content, but speed. When you feel the most stressed, how fast are your thoughts going? They're going at warp speed. The level of anxiety and stress you feel is directly related to the speed of your thoughts. All you need to do is create little gaps in between your thoughts. Even if it's for a few seconds at a time. As you do, focus on your breathing instead of your thoughts. Do this a couple of times a day. You can reduce your stress level almost instantaneously in *any* circumstance.

This next piece of advice takes a little more effort, but will be well worth it. Find periods of time, even if it's only five minutes at a time, and quiet your mind by meditating. At first, it may not be so easy to do. Stick with it. Pick up a book or a tape and train yourself how to meditate.

If the only change you make in your life for the next six months is resting your mind, you would see massive positive changes in every aspect of your life. That's a promise.

Now for the fourth and final element to our mental and physical well-being. This also happens to be my favorite. Giving ourselves treats.

I'm a believer in making healthy eating choices the majority of the time. Which means occasional treats are still on the menu. If I want chocolate lava cake (and who doesn't?) once in a while, I'm going to have it. If we deprive ourselves of pleasures too often, life is no fun anymore. That's just not cool in my book. So let life be fun for you. Don't be so obsessed and worried to the point that you don't allow yourself to have treats on occasion.

What works for me is sticking to healthy choices during the week. When the weekend comes, it's time for me to indulge a little. I may have wine, or a Cosmo (okay, maybe more than one), pasta, bread, ice cream, maybe even a good ol' cheeseburger, and guess what? It's okay. It's all about balance. If you go completely cold turkey and deprive yourself of what you love, your chances of sustained success are slim. So make better and more consistent healthy choices. Then when you want the cake, eat the cake.

Same goes for your mind. Am I a big advocate of learning and using our creativity? Absolutely. We need to exercise our minds. Yet, in addition, we also need to treat them. How do we do that? We make a conscious choice to let go of worry, even if it starts in short increments. We decide what makes us happy and allow ourselves to go do it. Whatever it is—night out with the girls, curling up with a great book, or watching a hilarious movie.

As sure as the laws of nature, your body, mind and life will give back what you give out. Same goes for relationships. Let's explore that next . . .

Lose this:

*Feeding your body and mind garbage
and pushing yourself too hard.*

Choose this:

*Feast on a healthy physical and
mental diet. Exercise and rest
both mind and body.*

9

◆

Relationships
are Easy

Happiness held is the seed;
happiness shared is the flower.
~Author Unknown

Have you ever noticed how some guys can't do enough for their babes while others seem to make it their life's mission to do pretty much the exact *opposite* of what their wives or girlfriends want them to do? Have you ever wondered why that is? Is it pure luck that someone lands a gem of a guy? Is it simply that there are only a few great ones out there and somehow, by some stroke of luck, some chicks just nail one, so to speak?

Here's another loaded question for you. Have you ever noticed how some guys (maybe yours) seem to fight you on everything but become putty in the hands of other women? All of a sudden, you see a person you don't even recognize—a person who seems to defy your wishes but who can't do enough to please someone else. Does that get your panties in a bunch or what?

So where exactly do we find the great guys? Do we go to the Good Guy Farm, where they put out only awesome guys? "Ooh, I'll take that one please. The tall one over there with the dark hair and nice tight ass. Wait, turn him around for a sec. Oh yeah, that's the one. Thank you very much."

Before I go any further, I just want to say that maybe the perfect mate for you isn't a guy. If that's what works for you, all the power to you. When I say *guy* or *husband,* I mean either sex. This book is about you finding happiness in life, in whatever form that comes for *you.* All the same happy bitch principles apply. Doesn't make a bit of difference, well, just one, but a few bucks will get you that. Anyway, moving on.

I have a lot of great men in my life. No one greater than my husband of course. That's a given, but I do. I love men. They're direct. I seldom need to analyze what they're saying to figure out what's on their minds. They come right out and say it. They don't whine (well, not much) and they are respectful to me. Men have a tendency to go out of their way for me, which means what? That I have a lot of influence with them.

Yes, I'm one of those so-called bitches you love to hate, and no, I'm not screwing them.

This then begs the question. Are great guys the exception to the rule? Or are most men a lot better than we give them credit for? I know that might be a little hard to swallow, but stay with me here. Maybe it's not the men. Maybe it's us.

If overwhelmingly, my experience with men is positive, maybe it's something *I'm* doing (or more important, not doing) that makes the difference.

That ought to be music to your ears. Why? If it is a practice of mine that is working, rather than the luck of the draw, that means you can have the same experience with men that I do.

I don't believe great relationships are totally based on luck. I think we create them.

If you are in a less-than-fantastic relationship, there are only two possible reasons.

The first is you simply didn't make the right choice for you, and time will tell, especially after you apply what you are learning here. However, don't be in a rush to make that judgment until you let some of what you learn go to work for you.

The second possible reason is you. Now chill out here for a second if you're feeling a little defensive. If your guard just popped up, and you're thinking "I do so much for my man, and he still does stupid shit. It's not me. It's him," all the more reason for you to be open to what I'm about to say.

Our behavior, actions, or lack of actions, beyond any other factor, have more impact than anything on the quality of our relationships. If we want change, we first need to look to ourselves. A happy bitch, one who has fantastic relationships with friends, co-workers, and significant others, attracts what she gives out. It's the answer that's right in front of us. Except too often we're so wrapped up in what the *other* person should be doing differently, we fail to see it.

It's much easier and much more common to blame other people or circumstances outside of our control. Except that is taking a position of weakness, a victim mentality. A happy bitch is not a victim. She's a powerful woman who asks in every circumstance how she can adjust *her* actions, behavior, or perspective to get what she wants out of life.

You may believe you already do everything in your power, and your man still doesn't measure up. The fact is, you probably have . . . *with what you've known until now.* This entire conversation is about opening your mind to new ideas. This is a big one, so listen up.

Have you ever heard a woman recite a list of all the things she does for her man and then bitch about how unappreciated she is? Can you hear it? "I can't win. I cook dinner for him every night. I run the kids around so he doesn't have to. I keep the house immaculate. He doesn't appreciate it. He's a jerk. I deserve better." Maybe these words have come out of your own mouth a time or two.

Maybe you do deserve better, but what if it's something else? What if without being conscious of it, your actions actually become a set-up to prove you are right about your observations? Subconsciously, there is a part of you that wants him to screw up so you can say "See! I'm right. I do nice things, and he doesn't appreciate it."

What happens then, is your life becomes a self-fulfilling prophecy. You believe it's all him, not you, so without even realizing it, you are on a quest to prove it. Proving you are right about what you believe becomes the motivation behind your actions. *Being right becomes more important than being happy.*

"I may be miserable, but I sure as hell am right!" Brilliant. I don't give a crap about being right. I choose happy.

You see, sometimes our minds play little tricks on us. We think that once we prove we are right, we will feel happy. Think about it. How long does the satisfaction of proving you were right last?

Do you want to know one of the most useless phrases ever? "I told you so." What does that get you? I'll tell you what it *doesn't* get you. It doesn't get you love, respect, or someone motivated to spoil you rotten.

How petty is some of the stuff we concern ourselves with? "He sits on the couch. He leaves the toilet seat up." So what? Is it really that big of a deal? Do these things really matter in the end? Making our point? Showing him who's right? Who gives a crap?

Sometimes on the mornings I leave the house before my husband, I get home to find the bed not made. I make the bed 99 percent of the time. Is it a lot to expect him to make the bed on occasion? No. Is it worth making a big deal over? No. How do I handle it? I choose to have fun with it. I call him up at work and say "You're not going to believe this. After you made the bed this morning and left for work, someone sneaked in and un-made it." What happens then? We both end up laughing about it.

What was the end result of how I chose to respond? Did I pull him closer or push him away? I pulled him closer. Always choose closer. Could I have nagged him? Yes. For what? Do you really think nagging motivates anyone? No. Are you motivated if someone rides your ass to do something?

Besides, think about some of the most annoying people you've met. Did they have a need to always be right? Bet they did. Guess what? The need to prove you are right is a sign of insecurity.

I know this seems like a small issue, but contrary to what many people think, most failed relationships don't fail because of one major blow. It's the little things, like a piece of sand in your shoe that grinds away at your foot, little by little until you can't stand it anymore. It's the clothes left on the floor, the toilet seat left up, the dish not put in the sink.

In the end, they are all insignificant. It's our reaction that gives them any significance, and who gets to choose that? We do.

You are an intelligent, confident, and capable woman. You are better than that. Not needing to prove you are right shows self-confidence, and self-confidence is hands down, the most beautiful, sexy feature a woman can have.

So lose the blame and finger pointing. It's a complete waste of time. It's choosing a position of weakness, as if you are a victim who has no choice. I don't play that ball game, and I don't want you to either.

I'm not suggesting you blame yourself either. It's not a question of blame. It's a question of finding the source of power to change. Which is where? With you.

That's the first element of my secret to great relationships. Stop blaming and look to yourself for improvement.

The next element is to make sure you know what defines his quality world and sing to that. You do that by really listening to him. Pay attention to the cues. What makes him happy? What makes him feel good about himself?

You want to pull someone closer to you? You want to have more influence with him? Find out what he really wants. Do what you can to bring that picture closer to reality for him. Then you become part of his quality world. You are someone who contributes to his happiness. It's not that difficult. In fact, it's easy once you see how this works.

I realize this is different than what you are used to hearing. Turn on the news, open a newspaper or magazine, and all we hear about are bitter divorces and how better than half of all marriages fail. Consequently, how many of us leave the starting gate half expecting marriage to be tough and not work out? We're used to hearing "Relationships are hard work." That's complete bullshit in my world.

Hit reset on your expectations, my friend. Not only do great relationships exist, *they are easy.* It's simply a matter of understanding and practicing a few fundamentals.

So back to his quality world and doing what you can to contribute to it. If you truly care about this person, shouldn't a major focus of yours be to enrich his life? To make him happier as a result of being with you? Yes.

Here's the deal. As you begin to concern yourself more with his quality world, *do so without keeping score.*

What I do for my husband, I do because the happier he is, the happier I am. That *is* my payback. Let me give you an example. My husband and I were in our sitting room off our master bedroom one evening. He said, "I need to go downstairs and get my laptop. I need to check my meeting time tomorrow morning."

I said, "I'll get it."

"You would do that?" he asked.

Why wouldn't I? It's little efforts like this that show him how important his happiness is to me.

Pay close attention to the motivation behind the "thoughtful" things you do for the one you love. Do them because you truly love him, and you want him to be happy. Period. Don't be nice to anyone, lover, stranger, friend, or anyone, if you intend to keep score. Your intentions are then misdirected. When your intentions are misdirected, the responses you get will be as well.

When your actions come from a place of self-confidence, love, and respect for the other person, that is exactly what you will receive in return.

A common misconception among women is when they feel they don't get enough from their men, they hold back, thinking the men will get the message and suddenly feel inspired to kiss their ass. Don't hold your breath for that one. If you feel unappreciated, and your response is to pull back and do less and less for him, what does he do? The same damn thing. Goodbye, happy marriage. Hello, family court.

When you know beyond a shadow of a doubt that you did all you could to make your man happy, you will either take your relationship in a much better direction, or if you do go your separate ways, you'll know you did your part. What else could you ask for?

If you're not sure what would make him happy, ask him. He will tell you. Then help him create that reality. Then you become part of his quality world. This is exactly where you want to be.

Can you see why women who find ways to prove their point (which serves only to piss him off) are shooting themselves in the foot? They remove themselves from his quality world and from a position of influence. Their goal is to get him to come around to their way of seeing things, to do, think, or act in a certain way, and the irony is, it completely blows up in their faces.

You know what else? I'll bet you anything, that not long after you ask him, he will ask YOU the same thing. Then what have you done? You just opened the door for *him* to ask *you* what he can do to make you happier. A heck of a lot more effective when he has asked you rather than you taking jabs at him "If only you would do this . . . If only you would do that!" We don't want to hear that ourselves, do we? We don't respond to that. Why would he?

Sometimes we just don't get it. We point the finger. We tell him he should do this and that, and he throws up a wall. Now, he will go against whatever you've pointed out, just to prove you are wrong. Is any of this ringing a bell?

It is exactly what I'm talking about when I say you get back what you give out. You are first giving him the opportunity to tell you what will make him happier, and he will respond in kind. It works like magic. You're going to tell him what he can do differently, but you are going to do it in a way that opens the door to make him want to do things differently. Did I say relationships were easy?

Okay, third and final part to my secret to great relationships. Stop trying to control him. Just completely knock it off. It's doesn't work.

Think about trying to control a teenager. How effective is that? The more you attempt to control, the more he or she rebels. Well, what are they really rebelling against? What it is you want them to do? Or the fact that *you are trying to control them?* Hmmm, maybe we're on to something here.

Remember how we talked about the driving force behind all we do? It is the feeling we expect to experience. How

screwed up is it that we think by engaging in unpleasant behavior of forcing someone else to do what they don't want to
do will in any way make us feel better?

Why do we do it? Especially with those we supposedly
love the most. Especially since it doesn't freaking work! You
may have short-term success and temporarily influence his
actions by bitching at him, but is he really internally motivated to make you happy? No, he's only doing what he's doing because he wants you to shut the fuck up.

What happens as soon as you are out of earshot? He
complains about what a nag you are. Well, are you?

Each time you attempt to externally control him, you
push him farther and farther away from you. Then one day
you wonder why you have no influence over him any more.

Get this straight. The only true influence you ever had
was when he was internally motivated because he *wanted* to
make you happy.

Wouldn't you rather motivate him by being a contributor
to his happiness, someone responsible for creating his quality world? Because guess what? When you do that, you no
longer need to worry about what he is doing or saying when
he's not in your presence. He wants to be good to you and
for you because you are to him. That's influence, my friend.

Why am I able to get along so great with men? With my
husband? I don't try to control them.

What are some of the easiest relationships we have?
Friendships, right? Do you want to know why they are the
easiest? Because we don't try to control our friends. We know

that if we do, they're going to high-tail it out of our lives. We realize we don't own our friends, nor do they own us, so we treat them differently. We don't own our men either. Just because they signed a piece of paper and said, "I do," doesn't mean we should take their presence in our lives for granted. They are in our lives by choice.

Why not treat your man the way you would your best friend? Stop trying to force him to do what you want. It's okay to let him know what makes you happy, but let it go at that. Give him the opportunity to *give* you what you want. How about telling him "I prefer you do this, but if what I want here makes you unhappy, I'll let it go. This relationship is more important to me than getting you to do something you don't want to do."

Which brings me to a crucial distinction in deciding what to take issue with and how to handle it. From this point forward, I want you to make your relationship more important than what you want for yourself. Got that? The relationship takes priority. It's not that difficult. Here's all you need to do, ask yourself this: *Is what I am doing or about to do going to bring us closer or push us apart?*

Choose whatever action will bring you closer, always.

By the way, to explore this concept of external control further, read a book called *Choice Theory* by William Glasser, MD. It is one of my favorites and loaded with powerful insight.

While we're on this topic of control, I want you to realize something. This control belief goes both ways. As long as you believe others control how you feel and what you do, you will be miserable. As long as you believe you can control how others feel and what they do, you will be miserable. Nobody wins the control game.

We fool ourselves into believing other people can make us feel a certain way or do certain things. We think we do what we do, react the way we react and feel how we feel because of someone else. This is the most disempowering and imprisoning belief of all. It completely relinquishes control over the state of your thoughts, emotions and life. Is that what a happy bitch does? Not even close.

No one can make us feel anything. We are way more independent creatures than that. We choose every single thing we do. We choose whether or not to feel a certain way based in the information we take in and how we process it—in every single circumstance.

Now let's talk about what control looks like. I mentioned it comes in many disguises. Some are obvious and some less so.

There's the obvious outright threats. "Do this or I'm out of here."

Recognize any of these? Blame, complain, punish, boss, criticize, nag, withdraw, pout?

What about guilt? That's a big one. I used it on my ex. I wanted to control his behavior. I wanted him to end his affair and choose to stay with me, so I did everything I could think of to make him feel guilty. What a dipshit. Me, not him.

I want you to always remember this. Power is the enemy of love. The more we punish, the farther away we get from what we want.

Ditch the blame. Understand his quality world, and become a part of it by helping him create it. Build him up. Make him feel good about himself and life, especially life with you. Don't try to control him. It's really that simple. This is true love.

Before we close this chapter, I want to talk to you about your search for that special someone, in case that is where you are right now. I understand that at times, the search can become all-consuming. Our worry about ever finding someone to share our lives with dominates our thoughts. We become worried, self-conscious, and depressed.

The catch 22 here is, if your underlying thoughts and emotions are of worry, neediness, lack of confidence, or even desperation, what will you attract? One of two things. Either another person who mirrors your own state or someone who will dominate and manipulate your weakness. You don't want either. Don't solve one problem only to create another

So what's the answer? You may be thinking, "I'm not happy alone. I don't want to be alone the rest of my life. My friends are all settled down. What if I don't ever find Mr. Right for me?" or "I'm older now. If only I had gotten divorced when I was younger, sexier or more vibrant."

The answer is simple. Surrender to what is right now. Completely accept that you are exactly where you are supposed to be in life right now. Use this time to just be you. If you are unhappy alone, finding someone to make you happy isn't the answer. That's giving your power away again. You may feel temporary happiness, but it sets you up for more intense pain. Why? Because you believe this other person is the reason for your happiness. You put all the power in his hands. So what happens if the relationship doesn't work out? Return of misery, unhappiness, and disappointment.

I want you to trust me, trust life, and stop worrying about it. All thoughts and emotions you feel are like radio waves, attracting the same signals. The moment you accept what is right now, peacefully, you create an entirely new sense of energy about you. I'm not suggesting you resign yourself to the thought that you will be alone for the rest of your life. On the contrary, once you release your resistance to what is right now, watch what happens. Chance encounters, coincidences, opportunities will cross your path and when they do, you now open yourself up to them from a place of contentedness, confidence, excitement, and curiosity. Not lack, neediness, and worry.

Maintain this sense of awareness and state of mind once someone does come into your life. Stay in tune to your thought patterns, because if you slip back to the worry of being alone or it not working out, you will have a tendency to cling too tightly to what you do find. What happens when we cling?

Imagine you're a kid again, and you see a brightly colored balloon. You want that balloon. You grab onto it and are so afraid of losing it, you squeeze it really tightly. Then what happens? You create intense pressure, and the air looks for the fastest way out. The harder you squeeze, the quicker it pops, and the quicker the air escapes.

Men are exactly like this. Believe me. I get that tendency to hang on. I've done it. I understand that it may feel counter-intuitive to not hang on to something you really want. I'm not saying to act like you don't care. Make sure he knows you want him but that you don't need him. Whatever you do, don't be a clinger. It is the fastest way to send your man packing.

I'll give you a perfect example. When I first met my current husband, I was dating someone else in an open relationship. He told me he was in the same position. I got the feeling before long that the other girl he was seeing didn't know about me, so I asked him. He was honest and told me she didn't. At that point, I was getting pretty attached to him. He was definitely the one I wanted to be exclusive with, but I had no interest in being the other woman. So, how did I get what I wanted, which was to see only him, and have him *want* to see only me?

Here's what I told him. "Look, I'm getting really attached to you, but I have no interest in being the other woman. So, go be with her, take your time. This is not a threat. I'm telling you right now that I really like you, but I don't think we should see each other for a while. I'm not going anywhere. I'm right here. I'm not looking for anyone else. Just take your time and figure out what you want."

His best friend's wedding was coming up that weekend. I told him to keep the peace for the sake of his friend, don't stir the pot and cause any potential problems for the wedding. Take her.

By the next day, his mind was made up. He chose me, freely, without pressure. So when he came to me, I knew it was truly where he wanted to be. Do you really want someone in your life on any other terms? They may be a part of your life and spending time with you, but you will always have an underlying sense of uneasiness, of being unsure. Why? Because you aren't 100 percent certain you are the one he *wants* to be with. There's no other way to truly have a fulfilling relationship. Guess who went to the wedding?

One final thought on relationships with significant others. There are some women who may feel a false sense of superiority to their guy and take advantage of him and his kindness. I have two things to say about that. One, you can't truly be a happy bitch by treating others poorly. And two, don't freaking do it. If you've got a great person in your life, appreciate him or her. If not, sooner or later, someone else will, and it's your own damn fault. Show love, appreciation, respect, and thoughtfulness. It's what you want in return, isn't it?

Intimate relationships play a significant role in our lives, but they aren't the only ones that are important to being a happy bitch, there's also . . .

Baggage Drop

Lose This:

Trying to control the one you love.
Worrying about being right.

Choose This:

Treat the one you love the way you would your best friend.
Help him or her create his or her quality world. Make
your relationship more important than anything else.

10

◆

Invite the Best in Others

When nobody around you seems to measure up,
it's time to check your yardstick.
~Bill Lemley

Unless you live in a cave or on a deserted island, your life
will be affected by relationships with all sorts of people. We
have relationships with lovers, ex spouses, brothers, sisters,
aunts, uncles, parents, children, in-laws, nieces and nephews,
co-workers, bosses, customers, clients, neighbors, friends and
strangers. A whole kit and caboodle of people who come in
and out of our lives. You know to varying degrees, they all
affect us.

What you may not yet realize is that the way we are affected by the people around us is up to us, not them. This is true for the relationships we have chosen to be in as well as the ones that come along as strings attached to something else—job, marriage, even family. Let's call these uninvited relationships.

The quality of our relationships depends upon who we choose to surround ourselves with, and also the manner in which we interact with other people.

First, how can we make the best choices about the people with whom we surround ourselves? I'm still amazed when I talk to people who don't even see this as a choice. They feel as if it is selfish or wrong to be selective as to who gets their time and energy. This happy bitch is picky as hell.

Second, how do we bring out the best of what uninvited relationships have to offer? Remember, whenever we're less than satisfied with anything in life, we look to ourselves and ask, "How can I change this?" It may be easier and more common to get caught up in focusing on what *they* should do, but all that will do for you is serve up a plate of powerlessness with a side of frustration—a dish you'll be eating night after night, because nothing changes until you do.

Let's start with the first question. "How can we make the best choices about with whom to surround ourselves?"

It starts with the recognition that you even have a choice—a choice that you should not feel guilty about at all. As a matter of fact, it should be a very deliberate decision on your part. Why? Who you surround yourself with greatly affects the quality of your life, your peace of mind, and sense of happiness. If you are around negative people who focus on what's wrong, who like to play the needy victim, who criticize themselves and others, do you think that will influence how and what you think? The types of decisions you make? How about the results you get? You bet your ass it will.

My sister, a very nice and thoughtful person, asked my advice about a situation with a friend. Her friend openly voiced her disapproval of my sister, insulted, and criticized her. My sister wanted my input on how to smooth it over with her, to keep the peace.

I said, "What the fuck for?"

"Well, she's my friend. I'm supposed to be loyal, right?"

I told her she wouldn't be the kind of friend I would have in my life, and I questioned if she was deserving of her loyalty.

It had not even occurred to my sister that it was okay to choose friends carefully. Her mind didn't question *if* she wanted the person in her life. Her mind questioned how she would keep the peace.

This is what you want to know first. Do you even want certain people in your life?

I like and *choose* easy, fun, exciting, and loving relationships. I like people who expand my mind, who want to grow and learn. I don't like spending time with people who are negative or criticize other people or who believe they are victims of society. If a friend has a bad day and needs to vent, that's one thing. We all have those days. However, when bad days become a way of life, when people create an identity for themselves on what is wrong in their lives and that's what they focus on, they are toxic. They're energy vampires, and they'll suck the life right out of you. No thanks. I'll pass.

I want people in my life who make me feel better, people whose lives I also enrich. I want relationships with those who value and appreciate what I have to say, who are fun to be with, and who are honest, genuine, and considerate of others. I don't want anyone in my life who talks negatively about other people. I want to be around people who don't feel the need to prove anything, who don't have huge egos and don't take themselves too seriously.

I don't want *any* relationship that is hard work. Relationships should not be work. They should come easily and naturally.

How do your relationships with friends make you feel? Do you feel relaxed? Do you feel empowered, supported? Can you completely be yourself without worrying about what you say or do? That's my biggest test. If I need to choose my words or actions carefully because I'm concerned about how you will respond, "See you later." I'm not hanging around you. I have zero interest in adjusting myself to be accepted by anyone.

Do that for too long, and you lose sight of who you are. You become a chameleon. "I better act like this with these people, and like this with those people, or they won't like me." Screw that. I like me. Take me or leave me as I am. I'm more than fine with that.

Here's a simple question you can ask yourself. Is your life better as a result of this person being a part of it? If the answer is "yes," that's fantastic. If the answer is "no," why is this person in your life?

I want to clarify something here. When I ask, "Is your life better as a result of this person being in it?", I'm not suggesting you look at every relationship and judge it by what you can get out of it. That is selfish. You will encounter good, decent people who at the time you meet them, are in need of love, compassion, support, and understanding. Maybe they need you to do something extraordinary for them. Maybe all they need from you is a smile. Your instincts will tell you what they need. If it feels right to you, by all means, give it to them. Sometimes what you get out of a relationship is the satisfaction of what you give. Sometimes your life is better, not by what the other person gives *you*, but by what *you give* her or him.

Start by identifying the types of people and relationships you really want in your life. Just as we discussed in Chapter 2, decide what you want. Decide what's important to you. Then take a look at the people in your life. Do they possess those qualities? If not, maybe it's time for some changes. Some people will fit into what you want in a relationship. Some won't. So what? Wouldn't you rather have a handful of high-quality and meaningful relationships than a bunch of shallow, unfulfilling ones?

If you decide it's time to weed certain people out of your life, remember this. Like you, they're doing the best they can with what they know, so be cautious of hurting anyone's feelings by telling them they're not good enough for you. Whatever you choose to say, or however you choose to handle it, just make sure to approach it from a place of understanding and compassion. As long as that is the basis for what you are doing, the right words will come to you.

Who knows? Your empowering choices just might rub off on them. As you learn and grow, maybe they will as well.

Now let's talk about how we bring out the best of what uninvited relationships have to offer? The question inevitably comes up when I tell people to be careful who they surround themselves with: "Yeah, well, what do I do if my family is screwed up?"

Guess what? Welcome to the club. I don't know any family that isn't at least a little dysfunctional or doesn't contain one black sheep they'd rather ship off to another farm. It doesn't mean there's nothing we can do about it. There are ways to influence their behavior.

At the very least, when you understand why people act as they do, their actions will no longer offend or upset you. Imagine being in that position.

Is there anyone who you don't have much of a choice about being in your life who bugs the shit out of you? Maybe someone who pushes your buttons, whose mission in life it seems is to make yours miserable? Perhaps a mother or father who frustrates or disappoints you, or an in-law or stepson whose demise you've secretly plotted?

What if you learned one nugget of knowledge that would completely eliminate their ability to upset you?

Sound impossible? Not only is it possible, it's easy. This is worth the price of admission ten times over. You are going to love it.

In the first chapter, I explained how many of us are unaware of the subconscious beliefs and memories that influence our behavior. Well, there is a twist—another element that influences what we say and do.

When someone acts out with anger, bitterness, resentment, aggressiveness, criticism of others, or is easily offended and defensive (any of this sounding familiar?), understand it is because they are partly unconscious. Not unconscious in the sense they aren't awake and responsive, but unconscious in the sense they are unaware that something else is directing their behavior. What is it? It's their ego.

Not ego as defined by being stuck up, conceited, or full or yourself. Put that definition aside for the sake of this discussion. I'm talking about something that exists in all of us to varying degrees. The ego is a part of us that among other things, is addicted to and survives on drama and negativity. When the ego is in control, in a way, the person has gone unconscious. It's not them talking. It's their ego. The ego does not want a solution. It doesn't want calm, peace, or happiness. These are all threats to its survival. It wants more of what keeps it alive and gives it strength: drama, unhappiness, and negativity.

The question for you is do you want to give it more of what it wants so it can continue to be destructive? It's looking to push your buttons. It's looking to get a reaction out of you. The more emotional your reaction, the more you strengthen the ego in the other person. Plus, once you react, the other person's ego has sucked you in. Then guess what? You just joined the club. You have allowed your own ego to take over and direct your behavior. The more you argue with the ego in the other person, the more intense, entrenched in his position, and defensive he will become. The ego digs its heels in and says, "Screw you! You're not going to win this."

Understand, when someone's ego is acting up, the only part of him you reach is his ego, not him. So why react? You're not getting anywhere, number one. And number two, you fuel the other person's negative reaction.

Think back on arguments you've either witnessed or been part of. They followed this pattern, didn't they? Have you ever reflected back on an argument and wondered how it got so out of control? It was ego vs. ego, both adding fuel to the fire. It's also why people lash out in anger and defensiveness and later are very passive and apologetic, not understanding why they acted the way they did.

Now you may be saying, "Yeah, but I'm not going to stand there and take their shit!" Well, let me ask you. Who is talking? Your own ego. That's who. How do you know? It's a defensive response, isn't it? The only part of you that has any insecurity or ever feels threatened is your ego. You no longer need to define it as "taking shit." You recognize it for what it is—a part of him that has temporarily taken over. It feels threatened and is in survival mode. It's searching for what will give it strength. Why feed it?

The only way a person's behavior can negatively affect you is if you take it personally. So don't. There's no reason to now that you understand where it comes from. This simple understanding releases any power his behavior had over you. His ego can't suck you in anymore.

If reacting emotionally and defensively is adding fuel to the fire, what is its opposite? What extinguishes the fire? Non-reaction. When you recognize and understand why people behave the way they do, that they aren't aware of it and often can't help it, you no longer take it personally. When you react calmly and without criticism, you'll see one of two results. They either stop coming to you for fuel, or when they do, the fire burns out because you're not feeding it.

When I say "non-reaction," I'm not suggesting for one second that you allow yourself to be abused. You can and should always take action to ensure your safety. What I am saying is there is greater power in responding in a way that is not defensive or argumentative. You can respond vs. react. There is a big difference. A reaction is emotional. A response is choosing how to handle the situation from a non-defensive, non-reactive position. A response is always more effective and powerful.

By the way, don't go pointing out to someone what you're learning here and try to show and prove to him that he is controlled by his ego. Even with the best of intentions. *Especially* if it is at the time he is acting out. He will see it as an attack on his identity and fight back even harder. Just recognize there is a part of him in control at that moment, and don't take it personally. Your non-reaction helps the situation and it helps him.

Should you want a deeper understanding of the ego, read *A New Earth* and *The Power of Now* by Eckhart Tolle. If they are the only other two books you ever read, your life will be transformed in ways you never imagined.

Now let's talk about how to actually influence the behavior of others. This is also simple. This applies to people who are close to you as well as strangers.

Do you think the vast majority of people you come across are miserable and unhappy? Be honest with yourself. If this is what you see and how you feel, it is a reflection of what's going on with you. Why? The signals you receive are consistent with the signals you give.

I won't argue that there are some genuine, certified jackasses out there. But the fact is most people are good human beings, with really great qualities of kindness, acceptance, understanding, and generosity. Besides, all of them are carrying around their own baggage and don't know it. They crave attention, affection, and a feeling of significance. Why not be the person who dishes that out, who lights up peoples' lives wherever you go? If that is the wave length you communicate on, you will attract the same in return.

This happy bitch does that all the time. I freely express positive qualities I see about other people, male, female, whomever, whenever. If I'm waiting in line or in an elevator with someone, I'm on the lookout for opportunities to brighten someone's day, to give a compliment on a woman's hair, handbag, dress, shoes, whatever.

I make a point to ask for and remember names of people I have just met. Then as I'm speaking to them, I repeatedly address them by name. Every waitress, bus boy, whomever it is. I call them by their name, I thank them for what they do for me, and I find an honest compliment to make.

Mother Teresa once said "There is more hunger for love and affection in this world than for bread." We all have a need to feel significant. Be clear on this: the best way for us to feel significant is to do our part to help *others* feel significant.

Send off little boosts of great energy wherever you go. If a store clerk asks you how you are, give her a powerful answer: "Awesome!" "Fantastic!" "Outstanding!" "Couldn't be better."

There are times people have stopped in their tracks when I reply like this. They're so used to "Fine. How are you?" Blah, blah, blah. Is *fine* what you want in your life? Or is *awesome* what you want in your life? Tune into a higher and better frequency. Send out fantastic energy, communicate to the world around you on that wave length and that's precisely what you will receive in return.

Granted, even with giving out the best of energy, we will occasionally come across miserable, unhappy people. If that is the exception in your life, terrific. They don't have to have any effect on you whatsoever. How they affect you is entirely up to you.

Most of us have grown up believing life will get better when the *other* person or *everyone else* changes their behavior. It doesn't work that way. Quit waiting. If you want people to respond to you differently, *you* need to change. I get that this might be a bit of a challenge to grasp. It means swallowing your pride and admitting maybe you haven't been doing all you could. BFD. Get over it. You didn't know then what you do now. From this point forward, enjoying easier and healthier relationships is in your hands. It's not up to chance. It's up to you.

Love, affection, understanding, and respect all have one characteristic in common. The more you give, the more you will get. The same goes for happy. The more happiness you give, the more you will get, which brings us to . . .

Lose this:

Energy vampires. Reacting emotionally to the actions of others. Waiting for and focusing on the need for other people to change.

Choose this:

Quality people. Not taking the actions of others personally. Invite the best in others by being the best you.

If you or anyone you know is in a relationship where physical abuse is involved, call the National Domestic Violence Hotline at 1-800-799-7233 or visit The National Coalition Against Domestic Violence on line at www.NCADV.org. No woman deserves to be physically or emotionally abused.

11

---◆---

The Perfect Drug

If you want others to be happy, practice compassion.
If you want to be happy, practice compassion.
~Dalai Lama

What if I told you I had a drug (legal, of course) that could alleviate sadness, cure loneliness, wipe away emptiness, and infuse you with instant energy, confidence, and happiness? Ooh, I feel an addiction coming on!

What if, in addition to being the perfect anti-depressant with zero side effects, this drug would also open a secret passageway inside you to untapped creative and intellectual abilities?

How much would you be willing to pay for such a drug if it truly did exist and worked exactly as I say? Imagine how many would give up their fortunes in an instant to possess it.

Let me share a truth with you. As sure as you live and breathe, the drug exists, exactly as I have described. No exaggeration. No bullshit.

So let me ask you this. If I knew where an infinite supply was secretly hidden, would you let me lead you to it?

Take my hand, my friend, and let me show you the way. All I ask, is you show the next person how to get there too. There's more than enough for all of us.

A number of months before I decided to write this book, I was having lunch with my friend Elizabeth. In passing, she happened to mention her daughter wanted to have a Sweet 16 party. She considered me a pretty connected person and wanted my input and advice on how to arrange it and whom to call.

This may sound like no big deal. Ordinarily, it wouldn't be. Except her daughter is no ordinary girl. Her daughter, Aiden, was diagnosed with lupus at the tender young age of eleven. Considering this child has endured nearly 50 hospitalizations, chemotherapy, physical pain, tremendous fatigue, and was once in a coma, it is a miracle she even made it to see fifteen. That, in itself is pretty amazing. But there's more.

This child has every right to be angry with the suffering she neither chose nor deserved. Who would blame her? As adults, we bitch and complain about truly minor annoyances that pale in comparison to what she's been through. But Aiden chose differently. She didn't ask, "Why me?" She asked, "How can I make a difference?"

Here's a kid, suffering from a life-altering and potentially deadly disease who sat for hours with the elderly as they knitted blankets for her to bring to children in the hospital. Here's a kid, who while in the hospital, told her mother to leave her side and go with her roommate, another child who was heading to surgery and had no mother with her. And here's a kid, who as she approached her sixteenth birthday, decided she wanted not just any Sweet 16 party, but one which would be a fundraiser to help other people afflicted with the same disease. *That* is no ordinary girl.

So there before me, over a cup of soup and half a sandwich, was her mother in an "oh by the way" fashion, asking my input on how to put it together. Unbeknownst to me at the time, that casual lunch would lead to a discovery that changed my life forever.

Not surprising, Elizabeth and her husband Dan wanted to support their daughter's wish. Except as parents of five children, a few of whom were in college, putting together an extravagant affair wasn't in the financial cards. While Aiden had dreams of a Hummer limo, the perfect dress, and a magnificent hall, they had to keep it reasonable and figured a party at a firehouse and a $10 cover charge would be about all they could manage. Or so they thought.

To this day, I don't even entirely understand, other than to just accept it was a call to action from some higher power, but something happened inside of me. It was as if another force took over, and I had no choice but to go along. Whatever it was, my mind rejected the firehouse idea, envisioned Aiden experiencing the evening of her dreams, and I sprung into action.

"That's not good enough," I told Elizabeth. "Set up a meeting with Aiden."

The way I saw it was this kid had endured enough already and was forced to give up more than any person should. (Go to www.BeatingLupus.org to read Aiden's story in her own words. Feel free to support her charity while you're there). If there was something I could do to help her family make this happen for her, I was doing it. Seriously. What would that say about me if I were able to do this and didn't?

A few days later, I was face to face with this very special girl. Here's how the conversation went.

"What I first want you to understand, Aiden, is that every single thing in life, this chair you're sitting in, this office we're sitting in, the car your mom drives, everything, first began as thought, as an idea in someone's head. I don't want you to worry about how. I just want you to tell me what your perfect Sweet 16 fundraiser would look like. For starters, where would you love to have it?"

"Well, I'd love to have it at the Grandview." Her face lit up as she spoke.

Mind you, the Grandview is *the* place to hold an event in the Hudson Valley. It is a spectacular hall with magnificent views of the Hudson River.

"Done," I told her. "What else?"

Understand I didn't have a freaking clue at the time how I was going to make this happen for her. No idea. I just knew that I would.

Aiden continued with her dream list, which included an SUV limo, her dream dress (which was a lavender gown she had already picked out), a DJ, fun lighting, purple balloons, a purple winter wonderland theme, oxygen bar, photographer and videographer. I just kept writing her wishes down and asking her, "What else?" Each time another idea popped in her head, she sat up taller, and her eyes became brighter. Never before had I witnessed so clearly the visible, physical results of empowering thoughts.

And for the final question I had for her:

"How much money would you feel good about raising?"

"I think $1,000." she replied.

"Is that all? Dream big, Aiden." *What was I thinking?*

"$10,000?" she questioned, tentatively waiting for my response.

"That's better. Let's do it."

I'll never forget what she said next. "This is the most excited I've ever been in my life." Take note here. Nothing had even happened yet. *She was excited, not by reality, but by thoughts and ideas.* What does that tell you about the power of thought? Her emotions, her actual physiology, were completely altered by only her imagination.

Was there risk involved? Huge. Not for my sake. Big deal for me if I screwed it up. My ego might be a little bruised, but

I'd recover. The greater risk was in getting this girl's hopes up. In retrospect, I think I had a bout of temporary insanity. If I didn't deliver, this kid would be crushed. How can you get her hopes up and then let her down? Only much later did I fully realize the risk I took.

I can't tell you why, but the possibility of failure never entered my mind. It was done before I began. I didn't know the "how". I didn't need to. When you see the "what" with complete clarity and absolute conviction, the "how" reveals itself. Nothing was going to get in the way of Aiden getting everything she dreamed of. It simply wasn't an option in my mind, so it never became one in reality.

Have you ever had a vision that clear? Convictions that strong? What happens? Dreams come true. That's what happens.

The evening of her party, Elizabeth and I stood in the spectacularly decorated ballroom (yes, the Grandview) in virtual disbelief of what we made happen. Wearing her dream dress and tiara, Aiden danced with her friends (all of whom arrived in a stretch Hummer limo) to the hottest DJ in the county. She, along with about every one of the hundreds of guests, climbed into the photo booth to forever capture the images of fun and joy, chose from a variety of fragrances at the oxygen bar, and ate three magnificent cakes made and donated just for her. Now a forever friend, Dr. Max Gomez, who ran two segments about her and her party on CBS News, toasted with tears in his eyes to her incredible spirit.

Toward the end of the evening, she stood before almost 300 people and cried as a young aspiring artist who flew across the country, performed a song he wrote just for her. A look out the window of the Grandview and the Mid Hudson Bridge's string lights aglow in purple in her honor completed the scene. It was nothing short of magical. If you're wondering if we hit her goal of $10,000, no, we didn't. We exceeded it. Aiden proudly gave away $16,000 that night. Together, we all turned a girl's imagination and dream into an extraordinary reality.

Not only did people donate their time and money generously, but they thanked us for the opportunity to do so. Why? They got something much greater in return—*the pure joy of lighting a fire in someone else's heart, of making another person's dreams come true.*

And there, my friend, is your perfect drug.

We get caught up seeking to acquire or accomplish what we expect will make us happy. I've done it myself. But when it comes down to it, the greatest joys come from what we contribute to the life of someone else.

From the moment I met with Aiden, something sparked inside of me. I came alive in a way I never had before. Every sense of taste, touch, sound, aroma, sight, and emotion were heightened. It was if the world around me suddenly sprang to life. It was the first time I had ever experienced anything like it.

I gave up about four months of my life and devoted virtually all my energy and attention to helping this special young girl. Some would consider it a sacrifice. Make no mistake, I gained more than anyone. All the money in the world couldn't touch the pure happiness I felt doing what I did for her. I felt overwhelming gratitude to stand there that night, to have been given the opportunity to be a part of making her dreams come true.

I saw Will Smith interviewed on Oprah once. There was one line he spoke that I'll never forget. He said, "You have not lived until you've lived in the service of others." That's a fact.

Think back on the times you felt the most excited, the most motivated yourself. Was it when you were engaged in something for your own benefit or for someone else's?

Life is not about the money, the prestige, or accomplishments, or selfish wants. It's about us having a sense of meaning.

You give me a person who feels lost and empty, and I'll show you a person lacking purpose and a sense of contribution. You want a cure for sadness? Get out of your own head. Quit rehearsing and replaying your own failures and problems and do something for someone else. There's your Prozac, baby.

If you think you're having a bad day, month, or even decade? I'll bet the farm you're playing the same tape over and over inside your head. You're stuck in an unproductive and unhealthy pattern of thinking. Your internal dialogue is reinforcing your shitty feelings, looking for and justifying all the reasons you have a right to feel that way. Get over it.

The fastest way out of despair is to look around you and ask yourself what you can do to make someone *else* feel better.

Here's my guarantee. No matter what you are experiencing today, there is someone worse off. Which means somewhere out there, someone needs you right now.

If life presents you with the opportunity to do something extraordinary for someone as it did for me with Aiden, my advice is to jump all over it. Dive in and give it all you got.

Along the way, you will find not everyone is in need of extraordinary. Calls for ordinary acts of kindness cry out around you every day.

An old woman whose family hasn't visited her in weeks sits alone in a nursing home. You pause for five minutes of your day and listen to her. Plan to go see her for lunch next week. Give her something to look forward to.

A blind physical therapist doesn't know the photo on his flyer doesn't capture his essence or the attention of customers. Don't stay silent and don't just tell him. Go take a better picture for him.

An old man stands in front of you on line at the grocery store. His tired eyes sparkle with tears when you hand the clerk the money he is shy for his food that week.

If you think I'm making these up, think again. No imagination required. They are all real life examples.

Look around you. Opportunities are everywhere. Your own feelings of sadness or lack will wash away the instant you lift up another person—every single time, without fail. You may not even need to spend a dime to do it.

Do yourself a favor as you help others. Forget keeping score. That's not the point. You may never see the person you helped ever again. It doesn't matter. You get your payback the minute you choose to spread love and kindness.

Here's what else I'll tell you. You may occasionally come across criticism in doing so. Fuck it. Do it anyway. I took some heat after Aiden's party. I'd be lying if I told you it didn't hurt my feelings at first. It did. But despite the criticism, I wouldn't change a thing. Nor would I let fear of future negative reactions stop me from doing something similar again should the right opportunity present itself.

When you get the chance to make a positive impact, go out there and give it all you got. Never mind any flack you might get. Unless someone has the balls to take a chance and do something as extraordinary as you do, he has no right to be an arm-chair quarterback. Screw it. The satisfaction and joy you will experience wards off any crap thrown at you. Duck and weave, baby. If you get nailed with a little, no worries. It's not going to stick.

We don't get a do-over. We do this thing we call life one time and one time only. When your ride is coming to an end, will you look back and celebrate what you did for yourself or what you did for others? Think about it. It's not that complicated.

One final thought for you. We are all here for a limited time, and so are those we love. If their time comes before yours, will you endure regret that you didn't do more for them while they were here, or will you carry peace with you always that you did well by them? The choice is completely yours to make.

I was incredibly close to my grandmother who lived to the age of 95. Do I miss her? Sure. Do I carry sadness and regret with me? Not for a second. There were times she needed me to literally fight for her survival when she wasn't able to do so herself. Then there was the time two nights before she died when all she needed was a kiss on the cheek and a spoonful of chocolate pudding.

Sometimes our opportunities to make a difference are grand. Sometimes they're as small as a spoonful, but they all count.

I also want you to know that if you hold regret in your heart right now for someone who is already gone, it's time to let it go. Go back and review Chapter 1 if you need to. Mistakes are life's little teachers. Use the lesson you've learned, and if there is someone right now who needs you, then do what you can now while you still can.

Let young Aiden be an example for us all. From the first few days of her diagnosis and the realization her life would never be the same, she chose to fight the disease inside of her with love and kindness for others. I believe it's a big part of why she's still here. How she views the world around her and her sense of giving back and care and concern for others *gives* her life.

The way we see the world around us is the defining difference between a life of regret and an extraordinary life, which brings us to . . .

Baggage Drop

Lose this:
*Being wrapped up in
your own problems.*

Choose this:
*Look for how you can enrich
the lives of others.*

12

$\blacklozenge$

Perspective
Determines Reality

*The real voyage of discovery consists not
in seeking new landscapes, but in having new eyes.*
~Marcel Proust

Imagine you jump out of bed one morning, heart racing because you realize you overslept. Of all days, this really sucks. You've got an important meeting, maybe an interview or big presentation you can't afford to miss. You jump in the shower, get dressed in a flash, and do your hair and make-up on the fly. Lips will go on at the stop lights.

You jump in your car, check your watch for the umpteenth time, and pray you don't get pulled over for speeding. About a mile and a half down the freeway, you see a long line of cars in front of you.

"Mother F'er!" You hit the brakes and slowly come to a stop. You are screwed. There is no way you'll get there in time.

How pissed would you be about now? We've all been in a similar situation at one time or another. Your stress level is through the roof. Out of your mouth comes a string of profanities you forgot you even knew.

As you sit there stewing, wondering why you have such shitty luck, you hear a rumbling sound coming from behind you. At first it's very faint, and you aren't sure what it is. As it gets closer and louder, you realize it is the sound of a helicopter. It flies directly over you and toward the line of traffic in front of you. As you look up through your windshield you see it is a Medivac helicopter. All of a sudden, it sinks in as to why there is a traffic jam. Someone up ahead is a heck of a lot worse off than you are. As a matter of fact, there's a good chance he or she may not be going home tonight, if ever.

So let me ask you something. Are you still pissed about being stuck in traffic? No. You're not. Is being late for an appointment such a big deal anymore? No, it isn't.

Let's look at what happened here. Your current set of circumstances stayed *exactly* the same. You are still stuck in traffic and will be late for your appointment. A minute or two ago, you were cursing the universe for screwing up your morning. Yet in a moment's time, you are no longer upset.

What does that tell you?

It tells you this. The state of our lives is *significantly* more a factor of our perspective than it is our circumstances.

With this one example, you can see how we are capable of completely altering our current reality simply by shifting our perspective. Imagine what else we are capable of doing. In how many different areas of your life can you do this? How about family, work, traffic jams, lines at the coffee shop, annoying co-workers, car trouble, missed promotion? In fact every single aspect of your life!

Get this and get this good. Your internal state is not defined by your circumstances. It is defined by your *interpretation* of the circumstances.

The implications go far beyond your ability to avoid getting upset in certain instances. *Way* beyond. You are actually capable of altering your entire reality—not only in how you feel about what's happening around you— but the actual outcomes you are getting in life.

When something happens to us through some sort of external stimulus or event, the results of that event are not necessarily predetermined. The outcome is heavily impacted by how we respond, and who decides that? We do. Always.

"I can't help but get upset. He makes me so mad when he does that."

Bullshit. No one has that much power over you. And if they do, you gave it to them. You choose your responses. No one else does it for you.

Jack Canfield, author of *The Success Principles,* uses a simple formula to demonstrate this concept: E + R = O. The "E" stands for the events in our lives, the external stimulus. The "R" stands for our responses. And the "O" stands for our outcomes. Bottom line, while we cannot always control the events in our lives, we do get to control our responses, which in turn affect our outcomes. Big time.

Now, the choices we make in how we respond are greatly influenced by what? Our perspective. The way we look at the situation determines how we will react or respond to it.

If you make a comment to me, and I perceive it as an attack on my character, I'm going to come back with something defensive and probably hurtful. If on the other hand, I recognize that your negative comment is a reflection of your own internal state and not a reflection of my character, I don't care. What you say will not bother me. I will not react negatively. I won't waste my energy.

Consequently, the more limited your options of viewing an event, the unhappier and more limited your life will be. Ever hear the expression "narrow minded?" This is exactly what it refers to.

Think about someone you know who is angry and bitter. Does he have a very limited view of the world? Does he have firmly embedded, limited perspectives and opinions? He does, doesn't he?

Who can blame these people for feeling the way they do? They believe they are victims of circumstance and feel stuck. From their perspectives, their options are limited or even dictated by something else. Therefore, the outcomes they realize are also limited—so much so that they feel trapped. What happens when people feel trapped? They fight for survival, for freedom. They attack. That's the anger you see, the criticism of other people and society.

It's also a classic underlying cause of women who are drama queens. They live as if their entire life's outcome is based on events, usually one event, whatever is happening at that moment. They're not capable of putting the situation into perspective, so they overreact as if everything rides on this one situation. Consequently, they end up screwing up their lives even worse because of their out-of-proportion reactions.

You'll also see narrow-mindedness in selfish people who don't share ideas, love, money, praise, or credit. Their limited views tell them there isn't enough to go around, so they better get and keep their share. Play that belief out. What does that manifest for them in life? Less and less. It's self-defeating.

Narrow-minded people think the key to their freedom lies in circumstances outside of them changing. The sad thing is, all that belief does for them is back them farther into a corner. They are trapped not by life, but by their own thinking. And they can't help it. They don't know any better.

The most ineffective approach to improving our lives is attempting to control our circumstances, especially when we do so from a narrow point of view. The irony is, it's how many of us operate.

The true key to our freedom, to living happily, to opening up worlds of opportunities, lies in our power to choose our perspective. The person with the greatest number of options of how to view a situation never feels trapped, and I can tell you from first-hand experience, this is true.

A couple of years ago, my husband and I were driving in North Carolina on our way to visit his family for Thanksgiving. It's about a twelve-hour drive, but we didn't mind. We decided to take our time and just enjoy the ride, which we did, until something happened that changed everything.

It happened so fast that it took a few seconds for me to realize we had just been in an accident. It was pouring rain. We were on unfamiliar roads and completely missed a stop sign. We took a direct hit on my side at 55 miles an hour, spun around a few times, and ended up somewhere off the road. It was surreal, like one of those bad dreams where you hope to wake up, and when you do, you feel tremendous relief.

Except this was no dream.

We were hit so hard my earrings flew out of my ears. I could barely see because my hair had whipped around so much it was in my eyes. I had pain in my chest and spine. Fearful of injuring myself further by turning my head, I slowly took inventory by moving only my eyes.

My jaw and left hand were bleeding pretty heavily. The passenger-side door was crushed in and resting on my leg, which meant I wasn't getting out of the car without being cut out. I was trapped.

Circumstance had its literal grip on my physical body. But guess what? What was I still free to do? Choose my response. I still had options, even though I couldn't move. I had a number of perspectives to choose from, each which would bring a different response and therefore a different outcome.

In that ever-powerful, almost magical gap between what happens and how we respond, is our ability to choose. It was never so evident to me than at that moment.

As I looked around, I could see that every part of me was still there, still attached. My husband was talking to me. He was alert and seemed unhurt. There wasn't anything else I needed.

Sure, I was uncomfortable, but I knew help would come, and I knew we'd both eventually be okay. I slowly reached for the scarf that lay in my lap, carefully wrapped it around my bleeding hand, and calmly waited for help.

The universe as my witness, I never panicked. I never even shed a tear.

That's supreme power, my friend, *and it lies within each and every one of us,* and in just a moment, I'm going to show you how to access it.

Before I do, let's talk about the flip-side, the opposite of the narrow-minded person.

Think about someone you love being around. She's inspiring, upbeat, and easy going. She seems to attract opportunities and good fortune. Let me ask you something. Does he or she have a pretty broad view of life? Does this person seem to effortlessly and almost magically help people feel better about themselves and their situations? Why do you suppose that is? I'll tell you why. Because he or she has developed an abundance of ways to view any given situation.

As a result, these types of people have at their disposal, the greatest number of options of how to respond. They have tremendous influence over their results and outcomes. They shape their worlds. The world doesn't shape them.

These are the types of people who live very full, rich and happy lives. They never feel trapped in a corner. They feel free and empowered. How do you do the same? Easy.

First, you recognize that there is a choice to be made. The choice comes between the event and your response. Your power is in your perspective, so the next step is to expand your available ways to look at what's happening around you.

The miracle unfolding before your eyes is realizing the world is not limited. The world is endless. It is abundant. Opportunity is around every corner, knocking on every door. It's hidden in every problem. The challenge is that each of us is looking through or operating under the constraints of filters. Many of them cloud our vision and limit our options. It's the difference between looking straight through to the bottom of a crystal clear swimming pool and a murky, muddy pond. Perhaps lying at the bottom of each is a treasure, but we are only able to see what is in the clear pool because of the lenses through which we look.

Each one of us, as a result of our upbringing and the factors I mentioned earlier, has developed our own set of lenses that shape and sometimes even distort our vision. We each have our own personal interpretation of the world from which we operate. Reality is very personal. It is shaped and dictated by our beliefs.

Take a religious belief for example. One person's interpretation of Jesus and the bible is very, very real to him or her. I'm not here to stand in judgment. I'm here to tell you it is a belief, and to them it becomes their reality.

Many of us live as if beliefs are a reality incapable of being changed or updated. We've never even questioned until now whether or not what we see as reality could possibly be a belief and more important, whether or not the beliefs we hold are productive or serve us.

Every belief we hold contains what was at some point, a positive intention. Something meant to move us toward something we want or away from something we don't. My ex-husband cheated on me. It was painful. I wanted to move away from and avoid pain. At one point, that belief served me. It protected me from emotional pain. But if I held on to that for the rest of my life, what would happen? I would live a sad and lonely existence.

I told you in the beginning we were going to do a little weeding. Pluck out some old, limiting thoughts and plant some fresh new ones. This is what I was talking about. Some of our thoughts are overgrown. They've taken over the fertile garden of our minds, and nothing else is able to grow. So let's weed and plant. Then welcome the harvest.

What are the weeds? Limiting beliefs. I'll sometimes ask a person to tell me a limiting belief she has, and she'll look at me with a blank stare. How come? She has never before recognized the difference between a belief and reality. She never knew beliefs can be changed or updated to better serve her.

So the first step in weeding them out is to uncover them. We do that by being on the lookout for any statements or thoughts that take on a cause and effect format. *This equals that*, or *this causes that*.

Let's look at how this shows up in a relationship.

"If he really loved me, he would marry me." This takes on a *this means that* format. To this woman, his not marrying her means he doesn't love her. Maybe he does. Maybe he doesn't. He may love her very much, but to him, marriage represents something different. But to her, this isn't a belief, it's her reality.

"He makes me so mad when he leaves his laundry on the floor." Here you see it in the form of *this causes that*. Her anger is caused by his act. That's her reality. But in fact, it is a belief. Her anger is based on her interpretation, on her chosen response to his action.

Let's look at how this applies to the criticism, disapproval, or judgments other people make of us. When someone criticizes or insults you, he is communicating to you the world in which *he* lives, not you. When you see hurtful or critical behavior in someone, it's a reflection of his or her view of the world. When you really understand that, never again do you need to feel hurt or upset by judgments and opinions of other people.

When I see someone driving like a jack-ass, tailgating, passing dangerously, flipping me or someone else off, it doesn't offend me in the least. I immediately recognize his behavior is a reflection of his views and beliefs, and I thank God I don't live in his head.

I understand that this concept of belief vs. reality may be uncomfortable for you. I'm basically telling you much of what you thought to be real may not be. Just let it sink in a little. As it does, you'll see how incredibly empowering it is. Your world is about to open up.

All that is needed is for you to change your frame of reference. In doing so, you will uncover and transform limiting beliefs. It's the power of reframing, and I'll give you seven ways to do it. You can use any one or sometimes all of them together in any given situation.

They are:

- Conspiracy to trust.
- Short sighted to long term.
- Obstacle to directional signal or feedback.
- Problem to opportunity.
- Blame to solution.
- Scarcity to abundance.
- Self-serving to win-win.

Conspiracy to trust refers back to Chapter 5. Rather than the tension and bitterness that comes with feeling as if the universe and others are in a conspiracy to make your life difficult, just imagine how different your responses will be when they come from a place of trust. Trust in life and the present moment. You will remove the vast majority of resistance from your life by doing so.

Short sighted to long term is exactly what it says. Ask yourself in a year from now or even ten or twenty years from now, how big of a deal is this? The shorter the time frame, the bigger the deal. The longer the time frame, the smaller the deal.

Obstacle to directional signal or feedback. When something gets in our way, when our plans are interrupted and don't play out as we expect, we get pissed off because the obstacle wasn't supposed to be there. Well, what if it isn't an obstacle at all? What if it is simply feedback meant to send us in a different and better direction, one that we hadn't seen when we started out? So the question changes from, "Why is this shit happening to me?" to, "Okay, what is this telling me? How should I change course here?"

Problem to opportunity gets your mind off of what is wrong with the situation and gets you in search of what good can come of this.

Someone very close to me, surprisingly young and seemingly healthy, suffered a stroke that threatened her life. She lay in a hospital bed for more than three weeks, the early days of which we didn't know if she would survive. While I would have taken her pain, fear, and suffering away if I could, recognizing I couldn't, I simply searched for the ways this could bring good to her life. I trusted this experience would give her the opportunity to live a richer life as a result. It has. Imagine the incredible value she now places on every moment she lives.

Blame to solution is self-explanatory. All blame is a waste of time. The second you recognize it rearing its ugly head, shut it down and think solution.

Scarcity to abundance simply means to choose your perspective and response under the assumption there is plenty to go around. Whether it is attention, love, money, whatever. Thoughts of scarcity lead to selfishness. Selfishness breeds more of the same. Thoughts of abundance lead to generosity. Generosity breeds more of the same.

Self-serving to win-win is a piggy-back off of an abundance mentality. The question isn't, "What can I get out of this?" The question is, "How can we all benefit from this?"

As you reflect back on the earlier chapters, you'll notice that much of what I'm doing with you involves opening your eyes to alternate perspectives.

The final frame of reference I want to leave you with is one that you will create. It will become your individual frame of reference for life and a source of comfort to you always.

It is your personal mission statement. It will keep focus, balance, and clarity in your life no matter what is happening. As the world and circumstances around you are changing, as they always do, you will have a constant guide, a part of you that always remains firmly grounded. It will become your personal constitution of sorts.

Not unlike our United States Constitution, it is the foundation from which all other decisions are made. Don't get hung up on the man vs. woman part. These words were intended for every one of us. What are the most well-known words from our Constitution?

We hold these truths to be self-evident, that all men are created equal, that they are endowed by their Creator with certain unalienable Rights, that among these are Life, Liberty and the pursuit of Happiness.

Even the men who drafted our country's constitution recognized our life's mission, our God-given right, is to live freely and pursue happiness. It's everything we've been talking about. Shouldn't happiness be an *objective* of ours, rather than a random by-product? We are meant to live with happiness as our intention. We need to give it serious consideration in every decision and choice we make.

Here's what I want you to do. Set aside some time this week. Give yourself at least an hour, more if you can. Look at each of the roles you play in life—wife, sister, daughter, mother, professional, friend, etc. Identify them and write them down. Then ask yourself in the largest context of time possible, temporarily fast-forward to the end of your life, and ask how would you have wanted to live each role? How will you want people to describe the way in which you fulfilled each one?

Then turn your answers into affirmative statements. This will become your personal mission statement. Please do this. Don't close this chapter figuring you'll do it at some point. Decide right now you will do it this week and schedule time for it. You will give yourself the most powerful frame possible. You will give yourself a set of lenses through which you will see the world around you in a way you never have before.

Life literally is what we make it. It doesn't matter what is happening around you. Even in instances where you feel hopelessly out of control lacking any power whatsoever—working at a job you dislike, illness, broken-down car, loss of job—you are in absolute and total control of how you choose to look at it and how you choose to respond.

My friend, you have a power inside of you that *no one* can ever take away from you. It is your secret weapon. Better yet, it is your magic wand. We don't always choose what happens in our lives. We do, however, get to choose how we view and how we respond to what happens.

When our friends and family learned of the accident we were in, their reactions were pretty similar "Oh, how awful." "That's terrible."

I choose a different frame of reference. This accident was a gift. In the whole scheme of life, it was a minor blip, really. But what it did was give us a greater appreciation of life. The EMS workers said we were miracles—that we shouldn't still be here. Our appreciation of life is with us every moment of every day. Whether we're washing dishes, flipping through a magazine, mowing the lawn, laughing our asses off at a funny movie, or doing laundry. We're grateful we still get to have these experiences. It has provided us with the opportunity to live a richer life. What greater gift could we ever receive?

I haven't taken being called a miracle lightly. My husband and I survived for a reason. There was more we were meant to experience and do—more we were meant to contribute. Maybe this book you now hold in your hands is part of that.

It's all about perspective, my friend. Nearly losing my life changed how I viewed everything around me. But you don't need to suffer something traumatic to be able to do so. It's simply the awareness there is a choice to be made and making it.

So the next time you're hung up in a traffic jam, be glad you are safe and comfortable in your car, and realize there may be someone who would gladly trade places with you. The next time you are annoyed at walking farther because you couldn't find a good parking spot, remember there are those who would give everything they have to be able to walk.

The quality of your life and the lives of those around you will improve greatly once you begin to learn to use the power of your perspective, which brings us to . . .

Lose This:

Narrow mindedness and limiting beliefs.

Choose This:

*Expand your available and empowering ways
in which to view the world and
circumstances around you.*

13

Be, Love, and Celebrate You

Everybody is a genius.
But, if you judge a fish by its ability to climb a tree,
it will spend its whole life believing that it is stupid.
~Albert Einstein

Have you ever felt like you were different than everyone else? In an odd-ball sort of way? I have. There was a time in my life I was convinced that somehow, instead of sailing along the conveyor belt destined for the "normal" bin, I got plucked off and sent to the reject pile until quality control could get their hands on me and figure out just where things went wrong.

Two days a week, Saturday and Sunday, and throughout each summer, I was brilliant and pretty. According to Mom, anyway. Then I would go off to school and suffer the wrath of being an oddity. Sucked for me, but at least one of my fourth-grade classmates was able to entertain himself at my expense. It didn't take much for him to completely annihilate my mother-deposited reserves of self-confidence. The only weapons he needed were a pencil, a scrap of paper and Scotch tape. Who knew elementary school was a cleverly disguised arsenal?

How could these seemingly innocuous items be capable of destruction? Easy. Take the pencil, draw a picture of a scar on the paper, tape it to your cheek and strut up and down the hall telling all the kids you are me.

Nice, right? What is it with people who choose to make fun of that which you have no control over? I didn't ask for the tumor on my face that required two surgeries to completely remove, or the ugly scar left behind.

I used to obsess over the other kids' faces. I wished my skin was smooth and perfect like theirs. Why couldn't my scar be someplace else where I could cover it up? Nope. There it was, right smack dab in the middle of my right cheek. I didn't need the word "reject" stamped on my forehead. The scar did that for me.

Did you experience anything like that when you were a kid? Did you ever feel that somehow you got gypped in personality, looks, or intelligence? Or that you were stuck with one or more physical features that left you feeling painfully different and inferior? It bites, doesn't it?

Despite all my mother's reassurances that I was special, pretty, and smart, I knew, deep down inside, I was a weirdo. Elementary school, or more specifically, dumb-ass Gregory and his pencil scar, proved it.

As I hurried out of the hall and into my fourth-grade classroom, all I wanted was to march up to my teacher and spill my guts so she would make him stop. There was only one problem with that plan. You don't dare open your mouth and try to speak when every last shred of your energy is focused on holding back a river of tears. I already acknowledged I was a weirdo. No way in hell I was going to become a cry-baby weirdo.

So I bit my lip and slid behind my desk, which, thanks to having a last name that started with "Z," was always the last seat in the back of the room. At times it irked me, but especially on that day, I was grateful for being the watcher instead of the watched. No one passed a note, fell asleep, or picked their nose without my knowing it.

I studied the back of Gregory's blond head and wondered just what was going through his little brain. That dweeb had ripped my self-esteem to the core. I wanted to crawl under a rock, run home, and never, ever go back to school again. Why would anyone be that mean?

My teacher knew why. At least she thought so. Pummeled for the second time that day on my way to the cafeteria for lunch, I finally mustered up the courage to tell her what the dumb shit was doing.

"Why, Mrs. Lynch?" I asked.

She looked down at me and smiled. Relief was in sight. She was about to see how wrong he was and make him stop. Thank God.

"Oh, it's just because he likes you. Pay no mind."

Note to self: *When I grow up, marry someone who puts me down and is mean to me. Then I'll know he really loves me.* Hmm, do you think we ought to stop telling our kids this?

That was it. "He likes you." It was the first time in my life it occurred to me that adults could be dumber than kids. I studied Mrs. Lynch the rest of the day, wondering just exactly when it was she had lost her mind.

After a while (which feels like a lifetime when you're nine), the kid grew tired of making fun of me. Now all I had to contend with was my unusually large big toe. How large? Big enough that your older sister names it Hammerhead. Christ, how did we ever survive childhood?

I beat myself up for about the first 12 years of my life thinking there was something wrong with me, wishing my physical features were more like everyone else's. I even hated my name because it was different. All I wanted was to fit in and be normal.

Until I realized what a complete waste of energy that was. I was trying to do the impossible. How so? Normal is an illusion. More than 90 billion people have walked the face of this earth. No two share the same DNA, fingerprints or big toe. There is no such thing as normal. We're all different—by design.

Yet look at how many of us struggle, sometimes painfully so, to fit in. "Fit in to what?" is what I want to know.

Have you ever wondered why so many of us fall into this trap? Where did this desire to be like everyone else come from? For many of us, it started at school. We faced pretty intense pressure as children to conform, to be like everyone else. We got picked on by other kids for not fitting in.

Interestingly enough, it wasn't just the other kids that made us feel that way. Even educational shows on TV had some unusual messages. Do you remember being shown a picture of three apples and a banana and being asked "Which one of these is not like the other? Which one of these doesn't belong?" What's the message there? Being different meant we didn't belong.

The questions ought to be "Which one of these is not like the other? Which one of these is *special*?" That would be a much better question to ask, wouldn't you think?

It's easy to understand why we grow up almost obsessed with the desire to fit in. We fall prey to the media, advertising, air-brushed models, and celebrities, telling us whom we should look like, what's hot to wear or the elite group you become part of when you drive a BMW or carry a $700 hand bag. The messages are coming at us from every angle—the latest shoe, hair, or dress style, what color is in and what is out. They even call them "must haves."

Is it really any wonder why we're still trying to reach an impossible goal—to be normal and like everyone else?

There is no law of nature that says you must be like anyone else but you. As a matter of fact, the laws of nature say exactly the opposite. Each and every one of us, you included, was created to be exactly as we are—unique. I don't care if you're white, black, yellow, young, old, gay, tattooed, pierced, have birthmarks, purple hair, or are cross-eyed. You are unique, and no one on earth, no matter how hard they tried, could ever be exactly like you.

Don't you think it's about time we embrace and celebrate what makes us special rather than hide and be ashamed? It's a complete shift in the way we learned to survive in grade school. And it's the most liberating new outlook you could possibly choose to take.

I've come to realize that I am supposed to be special. No one else out there has big toes quite like mine. That's not something to hide. That's something to appreciate. Forget worrying that we're not like everyone else. How about celebrating that no matter how hard anyone tried, they never could be exactly like us!

My unusual name that I used to hate? Now I love it. It's unique, *just like me, just like I'm supposed to be.*

And my scar? Well, it has faded significantly, but it's still there, and you know what? It doesn't bother me in the least. It's part of me, the whole package that is Keryl. In hindsight, it served me well. I couldn't count on my looks when I was little. I had to discover and cultivate other strengths. I needed to be smarter, sharper, and funnier to find a way to shine.

I look back now and am grateful life put me in the position to bring out those strengths.

Every day, you are being given the opportunity to shine brighter than the challenges or difficulties you face. Whether they be physical, intellectual, emotional, or circumstantial. It's not punishment. It's not unfair. It's an opportunity, another chance to shine, to reach deep down and reveal a greater part of you, a special talent or strength you never would have discovered.

Understand that you were put on this earth to be you. Not your neighbor, not your co-worker, not your friend, not someone you see on TV. I find it sad when I see people who instead of peeling back the layers and allowing their true essence to thrive, choose to conceal themselves, attempting in every way they know how, sometimes even including surgery, to be more like someone else.

Isn't that cheating on ourselves?

Judy Garland had it right when she said, "Always be a first-rate version of yourself, instead of a second-rate version of somebody else."

I may not have met you yet, but I do know this. You are an exquisite and unique work of art, an original, a living, breathing treasure and like no one else on earth.

You want to unlock the most precious secret to happiness? Discover the freedom to be you, to love you, to celebrate you.

It's so ironic the great lengths we go through to conform and fit in. Then what happens? We end up blending in so much, we become invisible. Is that really what you want?

I stepped off a train in Grand Central Station recently. As I took note of the mass of people walking ahead of me, all I saw was a sea of brown, black, and gray clothing. Everyone looked like everyone else. No one stood out. I smiled to myself because there I was, with the hottest pink scarf out there wrapped around my neck and flowing behind me. I didn't walk fifteen steps before a woman walking the other way, made eye contact with me, smiled, and said, "I love your scarf." I was noticed and acknowledged because I was *different*.

I want you to take a good look at yourself. Not just in the mirror, but deep down to your soul, to the very essence of your spirit. Everything about you is so special.

Believe me, the world is full of people hiding behind a façade or trait that they feel makes them different or inferior. Living that way will suck the life right out of you. It is not how the universe intended for us to live. Contrary to a lifetime of believing otherwise, the more you celebrate and love what makes you special, the more magnetic you will become. Think about that. It's the opposite of how most of us live.

When you find that magical code, where you accept, embrace, and celebrate you exactly as you are, people will be drawn to you. You will be envied and admired for your courage and self-assurance.

Look at Ellen DeGeneres. That is one seriously happy bitch who is adored by *millions*. She is one of the most beloved celebrities of our time. Her magnetism could pull the moon off its orbit. Yet, is she what we would call "the norm?"

Why do you suppose that is? Among other qualities, the biggest reason is she has learned to accept and love herself for who she really is. People sense that. People are drawn to that.

But it wasn't always that way for her. For years, she suffered the anxiety and pain of keeping who she was a secret, for fear of it holding her back or standing in the way. What did that get her? Prolonged unhappiness. Until she found the courage to bring her life in alignment, and then what happened? Her personal and professional life exploded. She decided to stop hiding who she really was, live true to herself, and accept the consequences. The rest is history.

Her appeal is mind-blowing, and it crosses all ages, background, and financial status. People identify with and admire her. They wish they had the courage to do what she has done—be completely and totally themselves.

It's not necessarily about going out there and flaunting your uniqueness either. If that feels right to you, go for it. More important, it's coming to terms with your true self, accepting and embracing who you are, and living in harmony between the you inside and the world around you. It's not necessarily about announcing to the world *I am anything*. It's about discovering yourself for who you really are and just being exactly that.

The pursuit of happiness is a fallacy. You were searching for something you already have. Happiness is within you.

It is something that comes *from* you, not *to* you. You hold the key. You carry it with you every day, in every moment and in every circumstance. The search is over, my friend. The fun, fabulous you is inside. She's been there all along.

Baggage Drop

Lose this:

The desire to fit in to an impossible norm.

Choose this:

Celebrate and be proud of the unique and special individual you are.

Conclusion

Often people attempt to live their lives backwards;
they try to have more things, or more money, in order
to do more of what they want, so they will be happier.
The way it actually works is the reverse. You must first
be who you really are, then do what you need to do,
in order to have what you want.
~Margaret Young

Well, my happy bitch friend, I have really enjoyed talking
with you. Before I go, there is one final story I want to share
with you.

When I discovered my ex-husband's affair, I had just given
notice that I was leaving my job. I had told only a few of my
co-workers what had happened. The majority of them, however, weren't aware of what was going on in my personal life.
On my last day, a few of them came into my office to wish me
well. Their thoughtful way of doing so was to have one of the
draftsmen create a huge going-away card for me. He was quite
an artist. There on the cover of this card was a sketch of me,
standing in front of my log home, with my fireman husband at
my side and our Dalmatian dog at our feet. I lost it.

I was looking at a depiction of my life, yet none of it
existed any more—not the house, not the husband, not even
the dog. That realization staring me in the face, losing everything I had cared about, them saying goodbye to me, was
more than I could handle at that moment. But not for long.

As I stared at the picture distorted by my tears, one image somehow came clear. Me, standing there, with my feet on the ground.

You see, when I said none of what was in the picture existed anymore, it wasn't entirely true. Standing strong, right in the middle of all the tears, all the uproar and change, was me. And you know what? I like me. I am a good, solid person, and I will always have that, no matter what is swirling around me—cars, houses, jobs, or husbands—no matter where I go or who I am with, I will always have me.

You will always have the same. No one and no situation can ever take your sense of self, no one can hurt you without your permission, nor can anything hold you back from your dreams unless you let it. You decide the person you want to be, or rather, you decide to let yourself be exactly who you are. No worries about acceptance or approval by anyone but you.

As the image of myself came clear, I knew right then I was going to be okay. Did it take a little bit? Yes, but I knew at that moment, somehow life would fall into place as it needed to. And it has.

I didn't know exactly how my future would unfold. I just trusted it would to my benefit, and I want you to do the same. In your toughest moments, I want you to keep the faith that all our challenges and struggles are put there for a reason.

Happiness is not something to search for. It's something to be. It begins by deciding to be the best you and love and appreciate who you are. All that takes is making choices every day that *you* feel good about. *That's it.* Will other people stand in judgment of your decisions? Always. Screw it. None of it matters when you feel right about the choices you make.

Will every decision you make be right? No. Has every decision I've made been right? Heck no. But every step we take, every experience we encounter sculpts us, teaches us, and brings us to where we are right now.

Will you experience a few bumps, a few bruises, a few twists and turns? Most likely. Just get your ass back up, dust off, and keep going. It's what a happy bitch does. You can't keep her down.

We women possess an incredible capacity to overcome the challenges life throws our way, and we come out stronger and smarter every time. Who we are is defined not by anything that happens to us—divorce, loss of job or loved one. None of it. We are defined by how we choose to respond—with grace, intelligence, compassion, and down-right, kick-ass determination.

This book may have been born out of my experiences or more importantly, my interpretation of my experiences, but it's all about you. You are the reason I wrote this. Let my mistakes, my experiences, good and bad, help you grab and hang onto the golden ring of happiness. Maybe it'll even help you prevent a few scuffles or battle scars. But if you run into them, don't worry. Deal with it, but don't ever question your character, your spirit, your strength, or your God-given right to be happy.

As you read the final words of this book, I want you to realize you have not reached the end. Quite the opposite. You have arrived at the beginning. Right now is the moment your new life begins—one filled with the ability to dream and the incredible power to choose.

What do you intend to do with that power? The way I see it, you and I have a greater responsibility now, knowing what we know. It starts with accepting responsibility for the state of our lives and happiness and choosing to live happily now. Yes, that is where it begins. But there's more.

What about the people who will come after us and those around us right now? The businessman sitting next to us on the subway, or the young mother standing in line in front of us at the coffee shop, even the elderly man driving in the car next to us. We are surrounded by people who find themselves trapped in their own minds and lives, desperate to understand how to set themselves free and live happily.

I can't help but believe that our quest to live happily must include enriching the lives of other people—by sharing what we know, by spreading the word of how to live happily. But even more important, I believe we have the capacity to greatly affect the lives around us simply through the manner in which we choose to live our lives—with compassion, an open mind, generosity, patience, and respect for each other. Regardless of our differences.

It's time to turn the tides of prejudice and judgment, of who is right and who is wrong. It's time for marriages, relationships, families, and a society based on acceptance and understanding. That doesn't happen by waiting for the world around us to change. It happens one person at a time, starting right here, right now, with you. What greater appreciation can you show for the gift of life than to use it to create a happier world?

It is my heartfelt wish that the new ideas, stories, and personal experiences I have shared with you reignite a spark of desire, hope, and faith in a place deep down inside of you—a place safe from any person or experience that may threaten its existence. Keep it protected, yes, but fuel it with courage and love. Let it burn so brightly that you carry the torch with you always and are able to share it with the next woman who so desperately searches for the answer to her happiness. For each time you light the fire in another, your own burns more brightly. Shine on, my happy bitch friend. May you hold happiness in your heart always.

The Beginning

About Keryl Pesce

Keryl Pesce is a Happiness Expert, inspirational speaker, radio co-host and entrepreneur whose insight, advice and wine have been featured in The New York Times, Bloomberg Businessweek.com, Huffington Post, Redbook Magazine and Glamour.com. She devotes her life to inspiring others to live their happiest lives.

◆

Visit her website at www.Happy-Bitch.com
to check out the Happy Bitch merchandise and
wine.

Connect with Keryl on Facebook at
www.Facebook.com/HappyB.tch
and Twitter as @KerylPesce

Made in the USA
Monee, IL
13 July 2023

39210464R00132